SHOPIFY

STEP-BY-STEP GUIDE FOR BEGINNERS TO BUILD YOUR ONLINE BUSINESS, CREATE YOUR E-COMMERCE AND START MAKING MONEY ONLINE WITH YOUR OWN PRODUCTS OR DROPSHIPPING.

Table of Contents

Introduction

Working for yourself in e-commerce is a great way to break away from the nine-to-five grind. It is not without its challenges, and it requires hard work. However, if handled with enthusiasm and dedication, an online shop can become an excellent side hustle or even a full-time gig. The only thing getting in the way of your eventual success is having the guts to take a risk and the fortitude to put in the hard work.

There are many platforms for selling your products online, but for the dedicated seller that wishes to work outside of other marketplaces, such as Amazon and eBay, Shopify is often regarded as the leading choice in all-in-one platforms. Additionally, for the seller that offers products available nowhere else, Shopify becomes one of many ways to sell directly from your own website.

If you're at all on the fence about starting your own e-commerce business, consider the perks:

- You are your own boss. There's nobody to answer to but yourself. For some, that may be a bit daunting, but if you have the skills for self-motivation and maintain high expectations of yourself, you will be able to meet your goals.

- You get to work from home. Don't you want to wear pants? Not a big deal. Want to take a break and go out for a beer? Not a problem.

- There's no limit to the amount of profit you can make. You will never hit a salary cap, and your job security will never rely on someone else's decisions. People have left jobs from all income ranges and became absurdly wealthier on their own than they ever could have in their previous positions; there's no reason you can't do the same.

- You won't get left in the weeds. As small, mom and pop brick-and-mortar stores continue to disappear across the country, online sellers are experiencing the opposite effect. Those with good marketing and great products are thriving by spending far less on overhead and attracting customers from all over the world instead of only catering to a small local area. Even if you do have a brick-and-mortar location, taking advantage of online sales is the only practical way to continue growing your retail business.

- Your shop continues working for you while you sleep. You don't have to man a front desk in order to sell products, and you don't have to get up early every day to make sure someone is there to help the customers. Your shop is always open.

Ecommerce is a great field for budding and serial entrepreneurs, and Shopify makes the process easier by leaps and bounds while offering what most of the other platforms simply don't. Their highly customizable and intuitive design elements completely eliminate the additional cost of having a website designed from scratch, and the platform is produced by a reputable company that has worked out all of the kinks already. Security is already built into your store, so there are very little worries about the potential of customer (or your) information falling into the wrong hands. Additionally, Shopify offers tools that help with marketing and analyzing your sales and profits, and they don't charge any fees for transactions. You only pay a monthly fee that fits the size of your store.

The first step is knowledge, and you're already on your way!

Chapter 1 Why You Need Shopify

With e-commerce developing into the biggest growth influencer worldwide, it is more important than ever to choose a solution that can turn your business into a better and profitable venture. Shopify in its basic form helps to sell your products and services on the web. Here are some solid reasons as to why you need Shopify for your business.

Simplified set up

In a traditional business set up, you would need to purchase an on-premise e-commerce software, which due to its standalone nature requires elaborate set up for IT and specialized development personnel, as well as management of the software. Such solutions had drawbacks like

- Expensive

- Not being scalable

- Difficult to use

- Time-consuming customization and integration with other processes of your business

Further separate software components are needed to take care of the front-end customer part of the business and the back-end operations such as inventory management, order management, customer service, and accounting. Bringing together the different software services to enable a comprehensive e-commerce platform hence becomes complex, with frequent need for maintenance. And this reduces overall efficiency as a result.

Luckily, Shopify provides the ideal solution by integrating all the important commerce requirements and business functions into one united platform through the SaaS model. Thus your business can create a relevant, personalized and engaging online experience. This is possible with Shopify's strong infrastructure that unites all the business systems and the information which feeds the systems.

Meet with customer expectations head-on

Your business can succeed only when your target customers can buy your services and products from your store online in an easy way. Shopify is unique in the sense that it can leverage and unify both the back office and front end apps complete with their shared and unique information. This unification of all systems enables easy visibility and meets with the expectations of customers in an effective way.

Success-oriented features

Some of the important requirements that Shopify satisfies include

- Unified platform: Has a unified accounting, e-commerce, inventory, POS, marketing, customer service, financials, merchandising and order management, which are managed via a platform that is cloud-based.

- Enhanced customer-centric operations: Personalized and consistent experiences for customers, targeted customer, and marketing service along with a single-window view of all transactions and interactions with customers at all channels and touchpoints.

- Smart order management: Increased profitability by having a single-window inventory and order management throughout all supply chain and channels

- Personalized customer experience: Fast, unique, compelling and personalized in-store, mobile and web experiences to highlight the brand value and surpass customer expectations.

- Enable unlimited expansion: Rapid set up of sites for various business channels, models, brands, currencies, languages, and countries under a single platform.

Streamlined comprehensive approach

To manage your vital business functions, you need a platform that provides a unified solution. It should encourage collaboration, align the operational processes and offer real-time visibility of data. Shopify meets with all these expectations and more. It helps control all the below functions in a cohesive manner:

- Analyses and reporting

- Customer support

- Procurement

- Inventory and order management

- Marketing

- Promotions and pricing

- Content management

Ecommerce platforms have moved beyond the basic unified software protocol to enable customers to buy services and products easily online. Shopify has excelled in this aspect with its competitive pricing and features. The e-commerce platform helps build a business that is easy to scale, fully customizable and offers a highly automated functionality that saves time.

In short, Shopify aims at providing a seamless online shopping experience across various different channels. The adaptability and flexibility provided by the software help to maintain the pace of your business, reduce the operational expenses, boost efficiencies and completely eliminate the trouble of managing software and hardware.

Chapter 2 The Features of Shopify

In this chapter, we will look at some of the features of Shopify, including the basic ones that most of the plans have, as well as some which are super useful, yet you may not have heard of.

Features on All Plans

All of Shopify's plans come with the following features:

• Unlimited products. This basically means you can upload as many products as you want to sell in your Shopify store without any restrictions.

• Unlimited bandwidth and online storage. This is an important feature as it means you won't be charged for the number of visitors your store receives or for the number of photos and files you upload there.

• Shopify POS (point of sale). This is a nifty tool that allows you to make sales at a physical store (be it a pop-up shop, a market, or fair, for example) using the Shopify POS app on your iPhone or Android. The app lets you process transactions in person and manages your entire store from your Shopify account.

• Online sales channels. This allows you to use multiple sales channels, including your online store created through Shopify and any social media accounts, such as Facebook. Everything is all seamlessly integrated so it's easy to keep on top of everything and monitor your orders and transactions across all your sales channels.

• Fraud analysis. This is automatically included in Shopify payments and it helps track down orders that could be fraudulent and alert you to this risk. This is useful for you to ensure all transactions are legitimate and to avoid potential losses.

• Discount codes. This is a great way to drive people to your store and build up a larger audience. You may have seen influencers on Instagram who have unique codes for their fans to use with certain brands; these are the kind of codes you get with the plans. Of course, how you distribute these to your audience is up to you. In addition to asking bloggers or influencers to promote your store in exchange for something, you can also give the discount codes to first-time buyers as an incentive to buy something and use the codes as part of a targeted email campaign.

• Overview. Every plan gives you a rundown of your key data related to your sales. This includes overall sales, how many visitors your store is getting, and how many orders are being placed. You also get finance reports that show you your income, your payments, and any pending transactions.

• Customer service. You can easily contact Shopify for advice, help, or tips on their 24/7 available support network. Shopify Lite gives you access to e-mail and a live chat whereas all the other plans have a phone number you can call.

Here are some features you get on the Basic plan. They are not available on Shopify Lite, but they are also a part of the Shopify and Advanced Shopify plans.

• Online store. The online store is a platform that you can customize to display and sell your products. Not only is it the view your customers get of your brand, but it is also the place where you can keep track of all the orders, transactions, products, and customer information related to your store. One of the best things is that it comes with a built-in website and blog, so you can run this parallel to your store and keep your products linked to informative, engaging content that helps tell your audience about what you sell, reach new customers, and get feedback on your store.

• SSL certificate. This is a useful tool that creates a safe connection between a browser and a server. This means that both your information and your customers' details are safe. By activating, it will show the little SSL padlock in the address bar which will give your customers a good impression and make them feel secure when shopping with you.

Features On The Shopify Plan

The Shopify plan has additional features not available on the Basic one that can really make a difference when it comes to providing a better brand experience for your customers.

• Gift cards. While discount codes are great, gift cards offer that extra bit more as they can be used on more than one visit to your site and store. It's also great to get new customers to your site, as your current customers can buy them for friends and family, who will then become your customers too. Shopify provides gift cards with various prices, so you can not only provide flexibility to your customers about how much the voucher is worth, but you can also customize the gift card to reflect your brand.

• Professional reports. These are great to help you understand the purchase behavior of your customers. These reports show sales of certain products to help you better organize the format of your store, as well as prepare for seasonal changes and plan ad and marketing campaigns. It also provides valuable information about who your customers are and how they interact with your store. For example, you can see the number of first-time visitors, the number of returning customers, who your customers are by country, and if purchases are one-off or repeated.

• Abandoned cart recovery. This is a feature that is definitely worth upgrading to in Shopify if it's within your budget and suitable for your business. In a nutshell, it automatically contacts customers that have placed items in the checkout but didn't end up making the purchase. By contacting them again after, you can encourage them to complete the sale. This is especially useful for stores with a high volume of traffic as this feature can significantly increase your revenue.

Features on The Advanced Shopify Plan

• Custom report builder. This feature lets you make unique, customized reports that let you really understand the activity on your site. For example, if you are paying for a specific ad campaign to increase traffic, you can make a report that will specifically track how that ad campaign is working for you by linking it to relevant sales and traffic. This can help you test the performance of marketing campaigns and create new strategies based on the data.

• Calculated carrier shipping. This is a great feature that lets you integrate third-party shipping services into your store so that not only are shipping rates exact when the customer goes to purchase, you also give your shoppers a selection of different shipping options including standard delivery, express delivery, and one-day delivery.

Features You May Not Have Heard About

The above features are the basic features that each plan, depending on its level, has. However, Shopify doesn't stop there. Here are some great features that you may not have heard about.

• Customer profiles. You can ask customers to create an account before they make a purchase. The advantage of this is that you can then track their transactions and see who your best customers are and what their purchases were. Why do you want to know this? This can help you to design highly customizable marketing campaigns for each of your customers, plan rewards for those who are most loyal, and send follow up e-mails based on purchases. For example, if a customer bought a daytime moisturizer from you, you can send them a follow-up e-mail near to the time when you have estimated the moisturizer will be finishing. This gives them the chance to make a repeat purchase from you.

• Shopify with Facebook. This is handy for anyone that has a big social media following. By integrating Shopify with your Facebook account, customers can purchase directly from there, rather than having to visit your site. It makes the purchasing process much easier and more convenient for your customers, which is something that can make or break a sale. Facebook also syncs all the transactions to your Shopify account, so you can easily run everything from one platform.

• Drop-shipping. You can use your Shopify platform to run a drop-shipping store, which allows you to sell products without purchasing any inventory. The way it works is a customer buys something on your store which triggers an order to be sent to a third-party supplier who then sends the customer the product they wanted. The customer will think the product comes from you – you'll be surprised how many online stores use this model – and it means you cut all inventory costs. There are apps, such as Ordoro, which you can use to manage a drop-shipping business.

• Future Publishing. To help you better manage your time, you can use future publishing to program content to be published at specific dates and times in the future. The content remains hidden until the date you have programmed it to appear on your site. This feature means you can program weeks' or months' worth of content to appear on your site which can help you organize campaigns better.

• Two-step authentication. This gives you peace of mind that your store is safe and protected from internet hackers who could steal your password. The two-step authentication means that even if someone did steal your password, it would be incredibly difficult to enter your Shopify account as you need to sign in with your account password and enter a code that is sent to your mobile phone.

In this chapter, we covered the key features that you automatically get with Shopify.

• Every plan comes with certain, basic features yet the number and sophistication of features increases with each plan upgrade.

• Which features you get depends on which plan you choose and this is completely dependent on what you need.

You can make your Shopify store even more functional with different apps that you can either get for free or pay for.

Chapter 3 Shopify Apps

The features that Shopify automatically comes with are great and can really help you build a successful and professional-looking store. However, when it comes to streamlining operations and adding a few extra functionalities, then you need to invest in some apps. Which ones should you get? In this chapter, we'll look at some of the best apps for your Shopify business.

To boost your sales or simply make your life easier by delegating tasks, adding apps to your store can make a world of difference. The Shopify app store is full of different apps which makes it hard knowing which ones to buy. Here are some of the best:

• OptinMonster. This is a great app to help increase sales and is also easy to integrate with your Shopify account. You can use it to show targeted promotions to specific segments in your audience, to reduce the number of visitors that abandon their cart and to improve conversions. It also integrates easily with any of your content management and email marketing platforms.

• Smile.io. This app lets you offer a loyalty program for your customers, so you can reward them for their purchases. Not only does this create a higher level of engagement, but it also gives your clients more personalized service. Best of all for you, it encourages repeat purchases which will help boost your revenue. With Smile.io, you can issue rewards for several different actions such as customers creating accounts if they share products on their social media accounts and if they start following your brand.

• Plugin SEO. Not only is this app amazing at what it does, but it's also free! Plugin SEO helps drive more traffic to your store by fixing your search engine optimization. It checks your page titles, the structure, and descriptions, among other things, to help troubleshoot SEO problems.

• Social Photos. In today's visual-heavy content world where platforms such as Instagram are becoming increasingly important for brands, apps like Social Photo is a great addition for your online store. Every time someone tags you in their Instagram photo using your product, Social Photo gathers these images and puts them into one gallery. You can then link the images to your products which can really help boost sales. You can also group photos together by themes and interact with your Instagram customers. This is a paid app and it starts around $10 a month.

• Facebook Live Chat Shopify. Gone are the days when waiting for a response from a company was acceptable; more and more people want instant interaction with a brand, especially if it's anything to do with a complaint or a question regarding an order. One of the easiest ways of connecting with your customers is through Facebook, especially considering it has over 2-billion users. The Facebook Live Chat Shopify allows you to chat with your customers on Messenger through your Shopify store and other social media sites.

• One-Click Social Login. This may seem something small, yet it is one of the most useful apps you can have to get your customers to make an account with you. Why do you want customers to have an account with you? Because then you can start sending targeted marketing to them based on their needs and preferences. Rather than asking customers to sign up with their email address and fill out a profile, with One Click Social Login, customers can create an account using their social media such as Facebook, Amazon, Twitter, LinkedIn, and several others.

• Printful. If you want to sell things that have specific designs on them, then Printful is the app for you. When an order comes through your store, it will be sent to Printful which will then print-on-demand patterns or designs for bags, posters, mugs, clothes and almost any other thing you can think of. If you're lacking in ideas, make the most of their design team who can help create incredible designs. After they have printed the design on the object you are selling, they will then send it to your customers. This means you don't need to hold any inventory or handle shipping as Printful will do it all for you.

• Aftership. Handling returns is a tricky business, but it doesn't have to be with Aftership, which can do it for you. Rather than your customer contacting you directly to return an item, they can go to your 'returns center' (i.e. Aftership) and send the items back through there. Aftership will also provide them with updates on the return and the refund. Best of all? It's free.

• Sumo. This handy app lets you collect e-mails and quickly grow your e-mail list. It also has smart bars, pop-ups and scroll boxes among other features that really help to build mailing lists and ultimately, higher profits. It also integrates with most of the popular email providers.

• Pinterest Buyable Pins. Pinterest has grown in recent months and is an increasing source of traffic and profits. Using Pinterest Buyable Pins, you can sell your products directly through Pinterest so potential customers can purchase without needing to leave the site. This is an especially useful app if you find Pinterest to bring your high volumes of traffic.

• PushOwl. This app is great for sending out notifications automatically to your customers. For example, it will advise them that there are discounts or items back in stock, as well as reminding them of items left in their cart.

There are hundreds of more apps for Shopify and many come with unique advantages that can really help you to reach and attend to your audience better and to streamline your admin tasks.

Chapter 4 How to Set Up a Shopify Store

If you want to have your own presentable, unique, and high-quality e-commerce store with all essential features, then you need to set up a Shopify store. Without a doubt, Shopify is one of the most popular online platforms that provide e-commerce solutions for entrepreneurs.

Shopify allows you, at minimal cost, to build a modern, functional, and professional-looking store all by yourself. The stores are very presentable and of great quality. They are very similar to what any professional web designer would build.

What is Shopify?

Shopify is a premier e-commerce platform that allows entrepreneurs to create their own retail point-of-sale systems and online stores. It is a comprehensive, complete, all-in-one online trading solution. Shopify allows interested entrepreneurs to open an account and set themselves up. Once you open an account, you can do all the following:

- Design and create your online store by yourself

- Identify a variety of amazing designs to choose from

- Choose a catchy name and domain for your online store

- Add then display products complete with descriptions and prices

- Start receiving and processing orders from customers

- Begin handling payments through various payment solutions

- Decide if to run any promotions, give discounts, and sell products

In short, Shopify offers you a very cost-effective and affordable opportunity to create your own e-commerce business. The software on Shopify is constantly upgraded to make it more efficient and modern which makes it more reliable in the long term. As an account holder, you get to receive excellent customer support 24-hours a day, every single day.

Key Features of Shopify

Once you open a Shopify account, you will gain access to a wide variety of tools. These tools will enable you to set up and manage your business. There are different pricing plans offered by Shopify. Depending on the plan you choose, you will be able to access a variety of tools ranging from payments processors to themes and so much more. Here are some of these tools that you will gain access to:

- Paid and free apps from the Shopify app store

- Paid and free themes that you can access from the Shopify theme store to ensure your website is exceptional and outstanding

- Shopify's own payment processor to enable you to receive credit card payments

- Access to a blog that provides you with articles that guide you on how to successfully operate and manage your own business and connect you with customers

- Opportunities to grow and expand your business

- Enterprise plans for high volume entrepreneurs who prefer lower transaction fees

- Global experts who can advise and help design and market your online retail store

Open an Account with Shopify

The first step you need to do is open an account. Visit Shopify's website at www.shopify.com and find the Sign-up page. Open this page and follow the stipulated procedure to set up your account. There are a couple of details required and once provided, simply click on the link that says "*Create your Store Now.*"

You need to come up with a unique name for your store. Shopify system checks all names you provide and only approves a unique store name. Other details that you will have to provide include your name, country of residence, address, and contact number. Shopify also wants to know if you have products you wish to sell and, if so, which products these are. Once you provide all the necessary information needed for setting up your account, simply click on the tab "*I'm Done.*"

If you are keen enough, you will notice that Shopify offers you a free 14-day trial once you open your account. This allows you to set up your store and test different things to see if and how they work without spending any money. At this stage, Shopify will require some details from you due to legal requirements. For instance, if you will be operating as a real store, then you will need to provide tax information and other relevant information.

Setting up your First Shopify Store

To set up your first store, you need to visit Shopify's homepage and look at the main dashboard. You will see plenty of buttons on the left-hand side. These include the following:

- Homepage button

- Orders

- Products

- Reports

- Discounts

One of the things that Shopify does is present you with an entire list of actions to take to fully set up, customize, and personalize your store before eventually launching it.

Shopify will then ask you what you want to sell. Simply choose one of the options available from the drop-down menu. These include electronics, computers, fashion, and apparel, and so on. Let us choose "Women's Accessories" like earrings, wristbands, and necklaces then proceed with this as our preferred niche.

At this point, you can start adding products to your store. The process is extremely simple. All you need to do is to click on an image then "drag and drop" it to the appropriate place on the dashboard. There is a button labeled "Add Product" button that you click on to add products.

You should label your products in a manner that clients can identify with. This also makes things easier for you when uploading or referring to a particular product. However, many dropshipping entrepreneurs do not have their own products and rely on a dropshipping supplier. We will look at importing goods from suppliers later. However, if the product images are readily available, then you can upload using this simple method.

Once you are done, just click the "Save Product" button then go to the homepage to view the products. These products are now ready to be viewed and even purchased.

If you visit the dashboard of your homepage, you will be offered a couple of options. Shopify wants to know where you want to sell the products. You can choose to create an online store, sell on Facebook, sell in person with a Point of Sale system, or even add products to an existing website. From these options, we note that the most viable in our case is to create an online store.

Find a Suitable Layout or Theme for Your Store

One of the most important steps when setting up your store is choosing an appropriate theme. Shopify has its own themes, and you can browse through them and choose one. There are plenty of colorful, great-looking, and presentable free and premium themes that you can use.

Now, all the themes at Shopify come with a guarantee that they have full support from designers. This is reassuring for users, knowing they can fully trust the themes. All the themes have a comprehensive array of modifications that you can apply without the need to do any programming. Premium themes have more functionality, but you can still do a lot with the free ones.

If you choose a theme but wish to make substantial changes to it, then you need not worry if you cannot program. Apparently, Shopify has an excellent team of design experts from all over the world. These Shopify experts are available to members and can help you customize and make any necessary changes to your store. There are some pretty simple steps to follow if you are to find the best theme.

1. Browse the Shopify Theme Store

First, go to your homepage and then click on the "Themes" button. This button will take you to Shopify's theme store at www.themes.shopify.com. There are over 180 different themes to choose from. These include both free and premium themes. When browsing through the themes, you can choose to browse through the free or the paid themes.

You can also filter the themes by features and by industry. The themes can then be sorted by popularity, most recent, and price. Spend your time browsing through the themes until you find a couple that really impresses you. Do not rush this process because your interaction with your customers will depend on your store's outlook and presentation.

2. Look at the reviews and functionality of themes

Once you identify one or two themes, check out a sample image. When you do, you will also receive more information about the theme including its flexibility, adaptability, and responsiveness. Additional information lets you know whether the theme is mobile ready and how adaptable it is to modification. There are always reviews if you scroll down, so go and check out the reviews. These will let you know about the experience of other users and what their thoughts are on a particular theme.

Shopify has a cool feature that allows you to view any theme you choose inaction. When you choose a theme, you will notice a "View Demo" button. Simply click on this button and preview the theme. This will give you a good feel of how your online store will look like. You can also view demos on the different styles if your chosen theme comes in a variety of styles.

3. Get your chosen theme

As soon as you decide which theme you like, you simply click on it to get it. You will notice a green button which you need to press. Shopify will want you to confirm that this particular theme is the one you really want. If you agree, then the theme will be installed. One advantage you have is that this theme does not have to be perfect. If you feel, later, that you do not like it, then you can always change it and choose another one. To install your chosen theme, simply click "Publish as My Store's Theme." Once it is published, Shopify will let you know and will offer you a chance to change it any time should you change your mind.

Top Free Shopify Theme

The theme that worked best for me in *Brooklyn*. It is among the most popular free Shopify themes available and comes in two different styles. These styles are Classic and Playful. The Playful style is more niche-oriented and features brilliant colors, making it suitable for kids' toy store, ladies fashion boutique, or even a chocolate store. The Classic theme is great for apparel stores and clothes retailers. It has excellent features, is user-friendly, and is very easy to use.

Brooklyn Shopify theme is well-suited for our modern apparel store. Some of its features include unique typography, a product grid, a homepage slideshow, and a mobile responsive design. It is not all themes that are designed to be viewed across platforms such as desktop PC, mobile, and tablet devices. You should not worry at all about products displayed on the theme as these are just for display purposes. You will get a chance to upload your own products at the appropriate time.

Edit Store Settings

You probably do not want your store looking like any other online store. This is why Shopify themes allow users to make simple yet effective changes that can completely alter your store's appearance. Consequently, you can rest assured that your store will be unique and stand out, depending on the settings that you choose.

First, visit your homepage and check out the admin screen. From here, click on "Themes" and you will see your live theme at the top. There are two dots next to the "Theme," both of which are settings that you can use. The first one allows you to create a duplicate of the current theme which is a great idea, so that is what we do. The other button is for customization. Use this button to customize the theme according to your preferences.

Simply click on the "Customize Theme" button, and you will be redirected to a page that allows you to manage all the basic functions of your Shopify store. These controls give you an amazing opportunity to adjust the settings and take a look at the features, enabling you to learn in greater detail what your store is capable of.

Customization allows you to change or do the following:

- Change font

- Determine the number of items to appear on each line on the collection page

- Upload logos to the store

- Determine your preferred color schemes

- Add slides to the homepage carousel

- Edit functionality on the product pages

With all these features and functions, you can easily make changes and adjustments to your store. This will make it unique, appealing and user-friendly.

Use Oberlo to Add Products to Your Shopify Store

Once you are done with the design and setup of your Shopify store, you now need to add products. For you to seamlessly import and add products, you will have to download Oberlo. It is the leading app used by e-commerce entrepreneurs who wish to import products to their stores. Shopify and Oberlo are seamlessly integrated, making it very easy to start importing and adding products to your store.

What is Oberlo?

Oberlo is a popular app from Shopify. It provides a useful service that enables you to import products from the popular

Chinese store known as AliExpress. As a dropshipper, Oberlo is ideally one of the best applications available to you. Using Oberlo, you can easily and seamlessly import thousands of products from AliExpress warehouse and start selling to your customers.

The reason why Oberlo is crucial to Shopify dropshippers is that it saves them plenty of time and effort when adding products from AliExpress. Oberlo is currently being used in more than 6,500 Shopify stores and has more than 300 positive reviews. Oberlo works only with AliExpress and not any other wholesale stores or suppliers. There are some very good reasons for this so let us first teach you a little bit about AliExpress.

What is AliExpress?

AliExpress is a global wholesale, and retail online marketplace developed and overseen by Alibaba, the world's biggest online marketplace. Anyone can place an order for wholesale items on AliExpress. You can also purchase a single item and still be protected by AliExpress Buyer Protection.

Buyers on AliExpress can purchase products directly from manufacturers. This enables them to get lower prices as they cut out middlemen. Buying directly from manufacturers ensures that buyers and dropshippers are guaranteed the lowest prices in the market.

Most people describe AliExpress as the retail section of Alibaba which provides a useful service to millions of traders, retailers, and customers around the world. Alibaba on its own generates more sales than eBay and Amazon combined. The term express means that this service is designed for express, wholesale transactions.

The main target markets of AliExpress include small and medium-sized buyers and suppliers. This way, they are able to access high-quality products at very affordable prices. The minimum order accepted is a single item or product which is shipped via express delivery. Sometimes fast and free shipping is available to entrepreneurs.

Sign Up for Oberlo

There are two different ways you can use to sign up for Oberlo. The first is to visit the official Oberlo website at www.oberlo.com and sign up directly. The other option is to sign up through Shopify. The Shopify app marketplace listing makes it easy to sign up directly. The direct access is apps.shopify.com/ali.

In our case, we have already installed Shopify on our device so we will click on the installation link that is provided. This link is highlighted on the homepage and is easily noticeable. Simply click on it and register. Once the app is installed, it will appear on your homepage.

From here, you can begin adding products to your store. We will need to register a credit card on Oberlo to do a trial run. Please note that Oberlo is not free to use. You get a 30-day free trial on the premium plan before moving to the lowest plan which costs $4.90 per month. For the app to be activated, you will need to approve this charge.

Benefits of Using Oberlo

- The Oberlo dashboard is pretty easy to use. It also offers plenty of conveniences. You can access the Oberlo dashboard directly from the Shopify admin section. On the dashboard, there is a section labeled "Get Started" that helps you accomplish certain tasks. For instance, it helps you set up pricing rules so that you know how to price your products.

- Oberlo has plenty of simple video tutorials that help you understand how to set it up. For instance, you can watch tutorials that show you how to customize products, how to import them to your store, and even how to connect existing products. Always keep in mind that your products form the most important part of your Shopify store.

- Using Oberlo, you can search for products at AliExpress. There is a "Search Products" page where you enter different keywords to find the categories and actual products that you want. Oberlo also allows you to import products to your Shopify store using either the product ID or product URL.

- You can also use Oberlo's Chrome extension if you want to import products as you browse AliExpress. If you are lacking ideas, then you can access a featured products page to get ideas. Sometimes you have to search through numerous products to find the right one. Each product comes with important information such as product rating, price, sales figures, supplier information, and so much more.

- Now that you have uploaded all the products to your store, you are ready to begin selling. Making sales and generating revenue is really what your Shopify store is all about. However, you will still have a lot of work to do because by simply launching your store, you will not necessarily attract any significant traffic. Therefore, you will also need to engage in suitable marketing campaigns to bring in potential customers. Keep trying different marketing methods until you find the one that works for your business.

Other Must-Have Apps for Shopify

1. Free Shipping Bar by Hextom

Free Shipping Bar is an app that provides a fully customizable bar. It enables you to offer free shipping to your customers to increase your sales. This app is easy to set up. It is not branded making your site look organized professional. It is an app that you definitely need for your store.

2. salespeople

SalesPop is a powerful tool that helps you boost your sales. It is estimated that over 85% of store visitors never buy anything. Reasons for this include store authenticity, trust issues, engagement and so on. SalesPop helps create an aura of a busy store that will entice customers to actually buy products at your store.

3. MailChimp

This is a useful marketing app with multiple applications. This app helps you capture emails from visitors and then create a marketing list. You can then use the list created to send marketing messages, newsletters, and so much more.

4. Personalized Recommendations App

This is an e-commerce app for Shopify that promotes sales at your store. It suggests the right products to customers based on purchase history and behavior. The app can tailor recommendations to every unique customer to your store.

5. Countdown Cart

This app helps create urgency in customers. A lot of customers tend to delay buying. However, Countdown Cart helps convince buyers to go ahead and purchase products at your store.

6. Trust Hero

This app boosts the level of trust that customers have in your store. When you have this app activated, it will display trust icons at your store and reduce incidences of cart abandonment. Customers will gain trust in your store and will be happy to buy your products.

There are websites like hotjar.com where you can create heatmaps and see how visitors are using your site. You can collect useful feedback which you can use to turn visitors into customers. It also enables you to know if your site has errors.

Chapter 5 Choosing A Product Category

Before you set up a shop on Shopify, it may be important to consider the types of products you can sell. In e-commerce, there are three basic product categories you can choose from, and Shopify is an excellent platform for all of them.

Digital Products

As you might have guessed, a digital product is something that can be delivered electronically. The largest perk of this product category is that it completely eliminates shipping, dramatically decreasing the time and costs involved in running your e-commerce store. The downside is that digital products often have to be produced, either by the store owner or by contractors. You can sell software from third parties as well, but the market is pretty saturated with this type of thing.

There are a large number of digital products you can sell, and a large part of understanding this market is either improving upon other such digital product concepts or providing something completely new. Some examples of digital products include:

- Sounds samples for musicians and artists to use in their music.

- Software for PC, MAC, etc. This can be the software you have developed, or you can work with software developers and offer their products. Note that selling certain software without a license from the company can violate the terms of service of Shopify.

- Web design themes (customizable!)

- Book cover designs (customizable!)

- Other design elements.

- Ebooks, music, and videos. Whether it is instructional ebooks and online courses for surfing or ebooks and movies about high-school-aged werewolves on the wrestling team, Shopify is an excellent solution for content creators in need of a sales platform.

- *Nearly anything that can be delivered digitally!*

Physical Products

Physical products are probably the most common types of products sold through e-commerce, and while the logistics are a lot more involved than digital products, this is likely going to be the path you go down. As long as the product is legal and doesn't violate Shopify's terms of services, it can be sold on Shopify.

The upside to physical products is that they are easier to sell. The downside is that you'll have to ship them, handle defective orders and returns, have a place to store them prior to sales, and worst of all, you have to purchase them before you can sell them, making the overhead higher than selling digital goods.

Common physical products include:

- Technology, such as computers, cameras, smartphones, video game consoles, and more.

- Media, such as video games, movies, music.

- Clothing items and accessories

- Beauty products, such as makeup and hair products

- Handmade goods, including customizable clothing and mugs, soaps, one-of-a-kind creations and basically anything you can produce

- Private-label products, which are mass-produced products with your own branding on them.

- *Pretty much anything.*

We'll go into more detail later about how to research what market you want to sell in, how to source products, and alternative methods of handling physical sales, such as drop shipping.

Subscription Products

Subscription products are a rising market as the likes of LootCrate and similar monthly subscription services have exploded in recent years. While there are subscription-specific platforms for selling these types of items, Shopify offers far more tools, customization, customer service, and reliability than these others. Also, there's no reason you can't use more than one platform.

You may have some experience with subscription boxes. There's almost one for everything these days. There are shaving kits that come monthly. There are candy boxes. There are gourmet meat boxes, clothes, video games, movies, collectibles... it is truly endless.

The huge advantage of subscription boxes is that you have an approximation of the amount of product you will require to fulfill your orders because people pay for the product before you even have to assemble the boxes. While you'll likely need to have some product on hand, you can maintain an inventory that makes sense for the number of subscribers you currently have.

One of the disadvantages is that you need to retain subscribers in order to make this business model work. This means a couple of things for you. First, you'll need to continue to source new products so customers aren't receiving the same things over and over. Second, you need to be able to create a perceived value that exceeds the price you charge. Part of the struggle with subscription boxes is that customers are often disappointed with the offerings for the price, even if they are more than fair considering all of the additional work that goes into putting them together.

With the growth of subscription boxes being offered, it is also worth noting that coming up with an original idea is going to make a huge difference in your success. If the same subscription box you want to curate already exists, the amount of competition can be difficult to overcome. That doesn't mean there isn't room for more strange candy boxes in the world, but it does mean you need to set yourself apart somehow.

As a seller of physical goods, it is obviously possible to sell a subscription box on top of your usual products, and this is a model that many subscription box companies have started to follow through with to hook in customers that may not want the experience of unboxing items they don't truly want but will purchase one or two of the items separately.

Choosing One

You probably have some idea which of these types of product categories you would like to work with. If you are unsure, it is wise to take the time to come up with a general idea for all three, handle some market research, and determine from there which are the most viable, which you are the most passionate about, and how easily the market is to break into. We'll discuss market research in more depth later.

Chapter 6 Extensive Template Options

The company provides highly professional templates that you cannot find in other e-commerce platforms. You can find more than 100 themes, which are offered free or as paid. Paid options range from $80 and go up to $180.The design and themes featured in Shopify are stunning and elegant. The numerous free and premium templates feature themes created by big names in web design including Clearleft, Pixel Union and Happy Cog.

Setting up

Once you choose from the various themes present, the next step is to customize the feel and appearance of your site. You need to just open Shopify's template editor. The steps for editing are easy to follow, so you can make the necessary changes until you are satisfied with the look. Once you have perfected the appearance of the theme, you can upload it by visiting the Theme page. On the page, you will have to click on the upload theme option. Your theme will be added. It's as simple as that!

Website customization

At Shopify, each website template has its own individual settings. This helps you to effectively customize the design of your website. The templates have certain key concepts, which are easy to understand and help customize your site efficiently. The important concepts in the templates include

Products

These form the base unit and are the core of theme building. The feature has several subsections such as title, its description, image, price and the variants like weight, size, color, etc. These and the product variants can be created and constantly updated through the online admin and the dashboard.

The variants form a powerful feature in Shopify. You can use them to display products in numerous attractive and appealing way in your templates.

Collections

After products, you need to classify them into various collections. This is necessary to categorize all the products successfully. The collections can be further organized in different ways such as alphabetically, by price, date or bestselling feature, etc.

Product tags

Tags add more information to the product and help in better filtering of the collection.

Themes

Themes help to increase the appeal of the store. Shopify has over 55 themes, which are available in over 140 styles. So you can have plenty of options to choose from when you are searching for the right theme for your online store. As mobile accounts for over 50 percent of all traffic in e-commerce, it is absolutely important for your store to be mobile responsive. Most of the themes at Shopify are of this category.

The editor feature in theme settings allows you to preview a template as you make changes in the template. This way you can have total control over how your store will look.

Expert help

If you are in need of a completely customized template design, Shopify design experts recommend you on the ideal template set up. The service has expert developers, marketers, and designers to advice on setting up a successful business online.

Without the hassles of hosting and web design limitations, Shopify provides a customer-friendly admin that helps you include all you have dreamed of about your store in a template. The professional features of Shopify further help you complete the set up in a full-fledged way. And one important advantage that Shopify has with regard to its templates is, you will not find any logos or ads in the templates. You will have to look very hard to identify that the site is supported by Shopify.

Best enhancing features

Shopify is an all-inclusive e-commerce platform that provides a comprehensive feature-rich solution for your online store. Once you have chosen a template from the Theme store at Shopify and improve the design, you can customize and optimize your site effectively. The Liquid template language enables easy control of template optimization, even if you do not have sufficient knowledge about CSS and HTML coding.

When you have optimized the template with change colors, logo and other features, you can start creating the product catalog with tools like Brand Names, Attributes, Categories, and Pricing. Promotions are also easier with the promotion tool, which offers automated discounts on products at a particular period of sale. After the period of promotion, the products will revert to the original price present before the sale.

Here are landmark features of Shopify

Design features

In web design, the advantages with Shopify include

- Professional and appealing e-commerce site, which is quick to set up and starts operating in minutes

- Customizable and compliant with standards free templates provided with the account

- Total control over CSS and HTML of your website.

- Liquid template language encourages dynamic content layout in a flexible way

- The facility of linking media assets to the entire shop or to individual products

- Forums and communities of Shopify designers to help with strategies and tips.

Content management features

The dynamic CMS in Shopify can help create web pages, blog posts, contact us feature and other features directly from the dashboard administration. It features SEO marketing tools and tools or coupon codes, besides having a full-fledged integral mobile commerce feature.

Order and pricing

The purchase features are highly efficient. Shopify provides secure payments via credit cards and PayPal via 50 payment channels. Customers have plenty of options for payments including eChecks, credit cards, PayPal, Google Checkout and much more.

The smart information collection features enable detection of the country based on the IP address. This will result in automatic changes in the currency, tax rates, language customization in the checkout page including the checkout at the shopping cart page.

Shipping calculators are also provided with Shopify. You can set up return and refund policies with the various order processing tools enabling a streamlined checkout process.

Background features

The infrastructural features in Shopify are well designed to ensure optimal data security. The PCI compliant Level I certification makes sure that customer information is guarded safely. With its open-source foundation, Shopify continues to tweak its features and improve them. The software is compatible with several direct payment systems and operates from a state of the art data center. Other salient features that reinforce the infrastructure of the e-commerce platform include

- Ruby on Rails framework

- Open SBD firewall guarded Debian Linus Server hosting

- MySQL database support providing speed and reliability

Point-Of-Sale

The POS feature in Shopify allows both online and physical location sales. When compared to competitors this feature has several enhanced items such as card reader, cash drawer, receipt printer, and barcode scanner. All these are available for purchase as an entire package or individually, according to your requirements. With an iPad, it is possible to use Shopify effectively to

- Sell from a stall in the market

- Pop up store

- Store in events

- Permanent retail outlet

The stock and inventory are kept automatically synced with the various locations, enabling you to manage multiple stores from a single point.

Chapter 7 Domains and Emails

Before your store goes live there are a few other details you need to deal with and the first is your domain name. When you choose one of the three main plans you get given a domain name but it isn't very exciting and it will do nothing for your credibility online. All that domain name consists of is your name followed by shopify.com. You need a domain that is going to scream your brand or your product from the rooftops and Shopify helps you to do this by letting you buy a domain name through a domain registrar. When you purchase through an external registrar, that name is yours for as long as you choose, even if you, one day, decide to move on from Shopify.

Use a reputable domain registrar, like GoDaddy. You will find that most offer much the same service but do your homework thoroughly and don't forget to read the small print!

Once you have chosen your domain registrar, type in the domain name you want and click on Search. You will see a list of the domain names that match or come somewhere near what you typed in. If the name has already been taken, you will need to think of another – tip: Before you go looking for a registrar, spend some time thinking of several names that will suit your business. It's highly unlikely that you will get the one you really want!

Your name needs to be memorable, not too long and easy to spell. People don't like complicated website names and will tend to move on to an easier one! You should pay no more than about $15 a year for a domain name if it is not a premium com or co.uk name – these will set you back a little more.

Chose which name you want and click on the "Checkout button" and decide how long a term you want to pay for. Longer periods tend to work out cheaper per year and 2 years seems to be the best bet – it's long enough to give your business chance to shine but doesn't tie you in for too long.

Input your payment and address details but be aware; if people search Whois for your domain name this address will show up. If you don't want your address made public, you can pay for an extra privacy feature on most registrars.

Once you have successfully ordered and paid for your domain name, you get a confirmation email. Click on the link in the email and you will be redirected to your control panel. Now you are ready to add that name to your Shopify site.

Return to the Shopify dashboard and click the option for the "Domains" menu. Click "Add an Existing Domain." Type your new domain name in and click "Add Domain." On your screen you will see a DNS address – write this down, you will need it in a minute. Also, write down the URL from the address bar – yourdomainname.myshopify.com.

In the control panel for your domain name (whichever registrar you chose), click on the option for "Manage Domains." Choose your domain name from the dropdown list and then go to the top of the page. Click on DNS and scroll through the list, click on "Show Advanced DNS Options."

Click to "Add a New Record" and type in the DNS number you wrote down – it must be exact, something along the lines of 205.95.223.56 (not this number!). In the Host box, type in your domain name, omitting the www from it. TTL needs to be set to 300.

Repeat these steps with CNAME and input your domain information.

It will take a while for all this to start working but, when they do, you will be able to use your own domain name to access your Shopify store.

Back in the dashboard for your Shopify store, click on "Domains" and then on "Set as Primary." Click on "Save" and you are ready to move on to the next step.

Setting up your Email Account

Now that your domain is all set up it's time to look at emails. You need a minimum of one email account for the domain name and this can be used for all your Shopify store contact details. Later on, you can set up one for each department or person in your business if you want. When you purchase your domain name, the registrar will likely provide you with one email address and a number of forwarders so what you could do is set up a primary email account and use other addresses to forward emails to that main account. If you need extra mailboxes, you can buy upgrades.

In your domain registrar control panel, click on "Email" and then on "Add New Address." Where it says Account Name, type in what you want the email address to be, sticking with a generic name for now like sales or mail. This becomes your primary address.

Next, click on "Add New Forwarder" and input the addresses you require, forwarding them to the primary email address you created first.

Once your email account has been set up, you can use any email client to access them, but the easiest way is to use the client supplied by your domain account. So, find your main email account and click "Login" beside it. Input your email and your password and then click on "Compose."

Input a message, with a subject line and an email address to send it to – use your own personal one for this test – and click on "Send." Check your personal email account to make sure the email came through. Reply to it and then go back to your domain email account to make sure the reply came through okay. If it did, all is working well.

Now we can move on to setting up the remainder of your Shopify store.

Chapter 8 Pages, Design and Payments

To set up the rest of your store, we need to create the pages you need, change the design of the site to suit you and add in how you will accept payments.

Creating Pages

We have a product or two in the store, we have our domain name and we have our email addresses. Now we want to make the store look like a proper store so we'll add some pages.

In your Shopify admin area click the "General" tab and go to the bottom of the page – a password is there, copy it and go back to your store webpage (the one with your domain name). Input that password.

Your store will look as it will to any visitor to it so look around, get the feel for it, click on stuff and make sure it all works. Once you have done that, you will have a better understanding of why you are going to be making the following changes.

We'll start with your front page; click on the prompt and you will go to your admin panel to the Pages section. Click on a page name and make some changes.

Input text as you would with any typing program. Give the customer a little information about you on your About Us page and also write what text is going to show up on the front page. Here, you can add other pages like a Contact Us page too.

Above the text window is a button for adding images; first, put your cursor in the position in the text you want the first image to appear and then click this button. Find your image (you should already have some saved on your computer for this). When you see the image in the window, click it and then click the box for "Size to Insert," choose the image size you want and then click the image icon again.

 You will see that your image is in the text area, but none of the text wraps around it. If you want your image to show in between two paragraphs of text then you can leave this as it is but if you want the image within the text, we need to change it so click the image again and then click the Image icon.

Input a description for your image and then click the option to "Wrap Text Around Image." Add a little bit of spacing around your image – this will show as the white space between the text and the image.

Click on the button to "Edit Image," and you will see the text wrapped around your image with a nice white space separating it.

Go to the bottom of the area for text entry on the page and you will see some more fields to fill in – these are to do with the search engines, which will list websites that relate to the text content searched for by search engine users. Provide a description and a title – this is what is going to be seen in the search results when people look for you so make sure it is specific to the products or service you offer. You can leave the URL as is or provide a new one that uses good keywords. Lastly, click on "Save" and then on "Your Website>View" so you can see how your page looks.

Have a play around with the features on here and try adding other pages to the site. Once you are happy with what you have and are comfortable with creating pages, we'll move on to site design.

Changing Site Design

Your Shopify store is starting to take real shape now, but it still looks a bit, well plain and boring. Shopify provides you with the tools to create a stunning looking website with little effort and much of that is in the form of themes.

Go to your Shopify admin area and click on the "Themes" menu. Then click "Visit the Themes Store." On the left side of the store, choose "Free" and then choose any of the images to see information about a specific theme.

When you choose your theme, try to look beyond what you see in the product description; try to imagine your own store with the theme. Click the "View Demo" button to see the theme in action.

If you like it, you can see what it looks like on your own Shopify site. Close down the demo so you go back to the theme store. Click "Get Theme" and then click on "Publish As My Shop Theme."

Next, click on "Go To My Theme Manager" and you can edit certain parts of the theme, like the colors and you can also images if the theme includes a header image or an image slider. Click "Customize Theme" and you will be directed to the Theme settings. As you make changes, click "Preview" to see them – this way you can decide as you go if your changes work or not.

You can add a logo and an icon if you have them on your computer. You can change colors, fonts and so on and you will find that every change is self-explanatory. You can change it back very easily if you find it doesn't work or you can even just go ahead and get a different theme.

When you are finished, click on "Save Changes." Don't be afraid to experiment and try several free themes. This will give you an idea of what works and what doesn't for your specific shop. If you feel like splashing out, you can also choose a paid theme. These can be filtered by industry and feature so you can find what you want quite easily. Do take care of choosing your theme though; it has to work and it has to do exactly what you want it to do. The alternative is hiring a web designer to create a custom website and that is not cheap.

Taking Payments

So, you have a fantastic store, filled to bursting with fantastic products and a stream of traffic just waiting to visit. All a waste of time unless you have a way to take their money and this is where we use Payment Providers. When the Internet first took off, the banks were too slow to come forward and offer good methods for online payments to businesses so, naturally, a number of other companies stepped up to the plate and filled the gap. These payment providers are what link the shopping cart to your bank. Check the Shopify website for more details about payment providers that work together with Shopify.

PayPal

PayPal is, without a doubt, one of the most tried and tested methods for taking payments, not to mention one of the securest and easiest. To use PayPal with your Shopify account you need to set up a PayPal Merchant Account. Shopify automates this so it isn't even necessary for you to have a PayPal account already set up. Shopify will let you know by email when a product has been paid for and to prompt you into setting your account up. If you do have an existing PayPal account, just click on "Edit" and input your PayPal email address.

Credit Card Payments

Not everyone uses or wants to use PayPal, indeed some countries restrict usage or don't support it at all. However, there are other options and one of those is credit card payments – for some customers, this is much easier and it can be more cost-effective for you as well. If you want to avoid a scenario where a customer abandons their cart before they pay for it, it is well worth considering using more respected providers, such as Nochex. If you are in the UK.

In terms of fees, here's how the Nochex and PayPal fees differ:

- *PayPal* – 3.4% plus £0.02 per transaction. On a £10 sale, you would pay £0.54 to PayPal, while £100 sales would cost you £3.60 in fees

- *Nochex* – 2.9% plus £0.20 per transaction. A £10 sale would cost £0.49 while a £100 sale would cost £3.10.

Small savings but, in the long run, it adds up to a whole lot of savings.

To set up credit card payments, from your admin control panel, click on "Accept Credit Cards" and click on "Select Credit Card

Gateway." Register your chosen service and use the same email address that you registered the service within the box provided.

Click on "Activate" and the service will begin working in your store.

It makes sense to offer a range of payment options to cater to all customers. Not everyone will want to add a credit card and not everyone will want to use PayPal either. Explore the options open to you in Shopify and choose the options that work for you.

Chapter 9 Search Engine Optimization

Search engine optimization is very vital when it comes to running an e-commerce store. It goes without saying that the sales of an e-commerce store largely depend on the ability of the customers to find it and from this point, make sales. So how do you increase your chances of being found and driving traffic to your website? Here are some tips that may help you with this:

- Do not solely depend on pay per click. This is a strategy that is used by a lot of e-commerce sites to increase the visibility of their stores. The dark side of this strategy is when one stops its implementation for traffic, the traffic can almost instantly disappear as well. Also, there is a mild feeling of distrust amongst customers when it comes to sponsored ads. While this strategy would pay off, one should also focus on implementing a strategy that grows traffic to their websites organically which is a better long-term strategy for maintaining their visibility.

- Do not duplicate content. Duplication of content on e-commerce sites whether in terms descriptions of products or even their listings may result in penalization by search engines. Therefore, it is important for store owners to look into the content they produce ensuring it is unique but also SEO optimized to increase traffic to their sites.

- Building a content strategy. Creating high-quality content that is unique will help your site rankings when it comes to optimization and will also prove a beneficial tool for encouraging repeat visitors to your sites since your customers will find value in your content.
- Refrain from using the product description from the manufacturers. Copy pasting this information from the manufacturer site in order to save on time is SEO suicide. Make sure to write new descriptions for your products which would help best optimize it and lead to increased traffic to the site.
- Optimize images of products. Image search increasing has become an important tool that users of the internet are taking advantage of to get products online. With this said, online stores should then use more keywords with the ALT tags from the images that they use. This helps their products to be found easier and this would consequently translate into increased sales.
- Include product review: Allowing your users to submit reviews for your products works to encourage the generation of content for better SEO optimization. This content, however, is being created by your customers and this saves you time and effort while improving your site's ranking.
- Have products linked from the home page. This is a mistake made often by many store owners. Their products are deep into their websites and what this does

is that it makes it increasingly difficult for customers to find your product. Furthermore, it adversely affects your product page's ranking making it harder to appear in engine searches.

- Organize the store for Search engine optimization. The manner in which you structure your store will affect its visibility. Think of organizing your internet store with the goal that it incorporates various landing pages of which they can be particular to a brand or item. Applying this structure affords you the chance to better optimize pages and keywords, which will build your site's visibility when they are looked up online.

One can also incorporate the use of coupons on their websites. What then this goes to do is that it will drive traffic to your website due to the increased interest. Including these coupons in websites and forums for coupons will also work to your favor by creating backlinks to your website and this will not only lead to increased sales on your website, but it will also go to increase your website's ranking on the search engines and consequently make it more visible.

Those are a few tips that you can use to improve on your website's search engine and consequently drive sales. I do hope that this information places you in a position that is designed to give you an upper edge when it comes to running your online store.

Chapter 10 Before You Go Live

Before your store can go live, there are a few more things you need to do, especially if your store is selling physical and not digital goods. Shipping rates need to be set, including postage and packaging and you need to let Shopify know how tax needs to be dealt with. You will also need to give your customers a way of contacting you in the case of returns or problems.

Shipping Rates and Order Fulfillment

To set your shipping rates, from your control panel, click on "Shipping." Input whatever locations and rates that you want but the easiest is to have two – a home country rate and then a "Rest of the World" rate.

Further down the page, there are options for adding Drop Shipping or Order Fulfillment. These are not Shopify services and are run by third parties – some of them very recognizable names. This is a great way of selling products across the whole world without needing to send packages yourself. You send the drop shipping company a load of your products and they do everything for you – storage of stock, packaging, and posting. And, because Shopify will integrate easily with these services, your sales can be handled by the other company without you getting involved in the order.

Tax Rates

If you earn over a certain threshold in most countries, there are tax or VAT systems in place. If tax has to be added to orders, click on "Tax" in the main admin panel and input the correct tax amount in the box for "Country Tax Rate." This will then appear on invoices and you will be able to see the tax you collected in your sales reports. If you don't have to collect any tax, this value can just be set as zero.

To see tax reports, click on "Reports" and then on "Tax Rate."

Contact Details

If you don't provide your customers with a way of contacting you, they are not likely to buy from you. So, on the main menu, tap on "Settings" and input your store details. All relevant email addresses must be included. Click on "Save" when you have finished.

Refund, TOS and Privacy Statements

In your main menu, click on "Settings" and then click on "Checkout" at the bottom of the page, you can set policy statements for refunds, privacy, and terms of service. To do this, just click on the button for "Generate Sample" and then use the generated statements or change them to suit your requirements.

Important note – make sure you do this ONLY after contact details have been input to ensure that the correct details go into the statements.

Payment Plans

Earlier we looked at the payment plans, now you need to choose one. By now you have had time to look at Shopify and see how it works and whether it will suit your business. If it does, go ahead and choose the plan you want.

Your store is now ready to go live. Check it over one more time to make sure and then remove that password – your store is now out in the wild and open for business.

Chapter 11 Shipping Methods

Throughout the book, so far, we went through a very large part that deals with setting up the commercial store online. We have learned all about setting up an e-commerce store and with that saw the things that we may require getting started. We have gone through the legalities involved. In our heads, we already analyzed the market and the products and settled on one that we were going to trade-in. Without shipping, without delivering the products to different clients, you have no business. Without being able to send your product from your storehouse to the clients, you cannot be involved in e-commerce. It would be more fitting to say that you are in the warehousing business.

Through this chapter, we will explore the different options we have when it comes to shipping our products to our customers and after looking at this we will be able to decide what option will be the best fit for our business and what will be the best fit for our customer base. Therefore, considering this, we need to decide what method we are going to use before making any order. We will need to go to the shipping settings on our store by clicking the shipping button on the admin screen to set up the different options. But before that, let us look at what they are.

The shipping methods and strategies you choose for your store will probably evolve with the evolving of your store and its growth. Among some of the choices, you will have to make, is what are the rates that you are going to charge for shipping. So below are some options that you can explore.

- Flat rate shipping

- Charge exact shipping costs

- Free shipping

Flat rate shipping

This involves charging a flat or standard charge for every package. This can also be varied to mean having a flat rate for a weight range, destinations of the goods or even the cart totals. When using this strategy, it is important to know the average cost of shipping to keep the price reasonable. This avoids undercharging that will eat into your profits and overcharging that will be exploiting your customer base. An example one can use for this type of rate is putting a $5 shipping fee for all the goods that are being shipped domestically.

Charge Exact Shipping costs

This method is just as is implied by its name, one charges exactly what it would cost for the shipping of the product from where the inventory is held to the doorstep of your client. For businesses in the United States and in Canada, Shopify goes a step further to help you out with this. One can take advantage of Shopify shipping and with this, they are able to display the shipping rates that are already calculated at checkout or your own customers. This is the best strategy, in my opinion for businesses that are still new and might be frugal with the funds that are available to them. This strategy has the customer cover their exact shipping costs and this reduces the financial constraints on the fledgling business.

Free Shipping

As suggested by the name already, this is a strategy for shipping where the business handles the cost of the shipping for the clients. Offering this option usually influences the cart conversions for your store in a positive manner. You might be thinking that this is impractical for new businesses that need to save up more and more of their limited funds to run the store but there are a few ways through which you can still offer free shipping to your customers in a way that is favorable to your new business. This can be by adding the shipping cost onto the sticker price of your product which would then insulate your business from taking an economic hit every time you ship a good for free. Another strategy one can employ is by giving free shipping on sales over a certain value of sales. This can be determined by either value-based or mass-based free shipping tolls.

Optimizing Shipping Rates

Being that you are now enabled to obtain rates that are already calculated for shipping from your store, it is important to ensure that these prices charged are accurate. This can be done in either one of two ways:

- Choosing to package

- Using product weights

Your store obtains rates on shipping depends on the weight of the cart and the size of the box the good will be shipped in. Adding the weights of all your products and the dimensions of the boxes that they will be shipped I would go a long way in improving the accuracy of this number. If this box is what is used for all your shipping, choose this box by setting it as the default making the calculation of the shipping rate faster.

Setting up shipping on your store

There are a few steps that can be used in setting this up from one's admin screen:

1. Enter the shipping origin of your goods

2. Add the shipping zones to it

3. Add the different rates calculated for the different shipping zones

4. If you are using Shopify to purchase your labeling, select the printer of the label and the packaging types that will be the store defaults.

Fulfill orders

The whole process that involved shipping your goods to the clients is known as the fulfillment of orders. These orders can be fulfilled manually by the owner of the store. A person can also involve carriers who will adjust the cost of shipping for the client and one can also use fulfillment services to ensure that their orders are shipped.

Customer Experience

After setting these settings up, a new store owner should test to see if the system and the application of the rates are precise by placing a test order to best get a feel of the customer's experience.

After a client has chosen a good, checked out, and entered their shipping address, the store consequently calculates the cost of the different shipping options that are applicable to them. The cheapest rate is what is usually set as the default and appears top of the list of the customer's options. In the cases of the customer retracting and changing their orders, their shipping rates are bound to change depending on the change in their order.

That is all there is to shipping and the different shipping options available to your customers in your store.

Chapter 12 Drop-Shipping

I am sure in your search for information with regards to making money online using Shopify, you may have encountered the words "drop shipping" numerous times and are just wondering, what exactly is this drop shipping and why should it be important to you who is interested in using Shopify to build your e-commerce store.

To answer your questions, dropshipping is a method of retail fulfillment where the store that is selling products and different goods does not keep any inventory of the goods they are selling. They do this instead by buying the product that is ordered and paid for from their online store from a third party and ship it directly to the customer. Through this manner, the seller of the good never gets to see r hold the product for himself as inventory.

The differentiating factor between standard retail procedures and models and the drop-shipping model is a seller never gets to keep stock nor holds inventory of the products he sells. In place of this, the seller makes his purchases from a third party based on the demand from his store. These purchases are usually made directly from the manufacturer of the products from different wholesalers. This merchant uses this strategy to fulfill his orders.

This model of running an online store has various advantages and disadvantages, and they include:

Advantages

1. Not capital intensive. This is arguably the single best benefit of a merchant who uses the drop-shipping model for his business. This model makes it possible for a merchant to set up a store and saving him the hustle of having to put up large sums of capital into the purchasing of inventory for their stores. In years before the emergence of drop shipping, a retailer had to use up a lot of their capital in the purchase of products that he hoped to sell.

Using this model, the only time that a merchant is required to make a purchase is after a sale of a product on his site. This serves as beneficial since the sale is already made and paid for by the customer. This then makes it easy for someone to set up an e-commerce business and store even though they do not have a large amount of money for this venture.

2. Easy to start. The operations of an e-commerce store are greatly simplified when a merchant does not need to deal with actual physical goods. Using of drop shipping as one's primary model alleviates them from having to deal with:

- Renting out a warehouse and managing it
- Packaging of your goods and dealing with their shipping
- Management and bookkeeping of inventory
- Dealing with returns on products
- Constant purchase of the product to maintain levels of inventory

3. Truncated Overhead costs. This is largely attributed to the fact that as a merchant, you are not necessitated to make purchases of inventory or similarly manage a warehouse. There are minimal overhead costs involved with drop shipping since many of these types of businesses are ran from home behind a computer using up under $100 every month as overhead costs. Of course, these costs are bound to grow with the growth of your business but they are still significantly cheaper than other traditional retailers.

4. Flexible Location. This type of business can be operated and successfully run from anywhere contingent on the fact there is a good stable internet connection. With the internet, one can maintain their contacts with the clients and the customers and with this, they are able to fulfill orders from their sites.

5. Wide Selection of goods. Since one does not require to put up money into the buying of stock and inventory, one is able to offer a wide array of goods to potential customers. One can add an item to their e-commerce store at absolutely no cost so long as the suppliers have them.

Chapter 13 Deploying Shopify Apps To Your Store

Start by Classifying the Apps into Relevant Categories

Brilliant developers from across the globe have contributed more than 500 apps to Shopify Apps Store over the years. These apps are designed to extend the core functionalities of Shopify stores. In other words, they will make your store to do things it could never do otherwise. Unfortunately picking the *right* apps for your store can become an overwhelming task when you're just starting out. No thanks to the fact that you may have to sieve through a plethora of options. To avoid getting overwhelmed when choosing apps, I usually advise new Shopify merchants to first define the extended functions they'd like to deploy on their stores. And one way to do that is to lump the apps into various categories. Here's an example of such categorization:

1. Operations Management Apps

Operations Apps will help to make the day to day operation of your store way easier. Here's an example of apps you may add to this category:

• *Inventory Management App* (if your store is stocking its products in real-time)

- *Shipping/Labeling Apps* (if you ship tangible products directly to your customers)

- *Drop Shipping/Fulfillment Apps* (if your stores don't maintain inventory nor fulfill orders)

- *Accounting App* (if you want to sync your online store with your accounting software)

- *Reporting and Analytic Apps* (To collect data and help you make better decisions)

2. User Experience (UX) and Interaction Apps
These are apps that help to make your customers say "wow" when they interact with your store. Examples of UX and interaction apps may include the following:

- *Live Chat Apps* (to connect with your customers in real-time)

- *Customer Relationship Management/Personalization Apps* (for the sense of belonging)

- *Notifications/Suggestions/Quizzes/Alerts Apps* (to make your store appear smart)

- *Language Translation Apps* (if your shop serves people who speak different languages)

- *Speed Enhancement Apps* (to make your store load faster than light, if possible)

- *Image Optimization Apps* (to give your product images a larger than life effect)

3. Promotions Apps

These are apps that would help you attract visitors to your store, convert them to leads, nurture them as prospects and turn them to paying customers and your brand's evangelists. Here are some apps that may be included in this category:

- *SEO Apps* (to help endear your store to the search engines)

- *Email Marketing Apps* (to help fuse your store visitors into your sales funnel)

- *Blog Apps* (to engage your visitors better and steer them in the right direction)

- *Syndication Apps* (to push your inventory to third party shopping engines via RSS)

- *Social Proof Apps* (to build customer reviews and user-generated contents)

- *Coupon Apps* (to bribe your visitors into buying more or opting into your sales funnel)

4. Sales Channel Apps

These are apps that help you expand your storefront across multiple channels in the digital space. Think of it as establishing a chain of stores in your country or region. Some apps that may be included in this category are:

• *Web Store App* (Well, this is where it all begins. Just expand to other channels from here)

• *Social Media Store Apps* (to extend your store to Facebook, Twitter, Pinterest, etc).

• *Mobile Store Apps* (to make your whole store available as a mobile app)

Of course, this whole concept of Shopify apps classification is entirely unique to this book. And that's a nice way to say that you may not find it exactly the same way elsewhere; and certainly not anywhere on Shopify. What we're doing here is just to give you a structural idea of what you may choose to look for when you go through the Shopify app store.

Some Recommended Third-Party Apps/Services

Wow, it's come to that point where I just have to stick out my neck and literally mention specific apps/services by their names. But of course, you should remember that you're still at the *experimentation* stage in your eCommerce journey. I guess that's why you read this book. So I'm not in any way suggesting that you should go for **all** the recommended third-party apps/services right out of the box. On the contrary, I'm saying you shouldn't. The recommendations are only intended to show you a bit of the good stuff so you can make informed buying decisions when you reach the *certainty* stage in your eCommerce journey.

And of course, you should also understand that although the following recommendations are based on my hands-on experience and informed opinion on Shopify, yet that doesn't make this list the last word on Shopify apps role call. So it's very likely that there are other amazing apps out there that are not included on the list. My gosh, we're talking about well over 500 apps here. But below is a handful of apps you're likely to fall in love with.

Recommended Operations Management Apps/Services

App/Service Name: Ordoro

Function: Inventory, Shipping, and Dropshipping Management

Price: From $99/Month

Ordoro is actually a third party full-scale *shipping* service in its core, but it also features a full-stack *inventory* and *dropshipping* management system. The amazing thing about this app is that it efficiently integrates with lots of other super eCommerce services in addition to Shopify. Just look at it as your central business hub that connects your store, and manages all of its inventories, across various major *eCommerce platforms* (like Shopify, eBay, Amazon, Etsy, WooCommerce,

Bigcommerce, etc., *all at the same time*). The app also connects your store to shippers (like UPS, FedEx, etc.), drop shippers (like Fulfillment by Amazon) and accounting services (like QuickBooks, etc.), and many other services. And it's all done with the ease of mouse clicks. And if you have any service that's not listed for integration, there are chances that you can also integrate those successfully with Ordoro's *open API* system.

The downside of this app, however, is that it may just be too loaded for a small store that's just starting out. And unless you also plan to (at least) ship some of your products personally, you may find that you are paying way too much for services you don't even use or need.

Quick Tip: Many new merchants (except the big brick and mortar stores) that are just looking to test their feet in eCommerce can do well without this app. You may find that the native Shopify inventory management system (though more tedious) offers most of what you need for now. You may just have to prop it up a little bit with a few *inventory alert apps* that'd warn you and your customers when products are going down or have gone completely out of stock. You may also use smaller *shipping or dropshipping apps* that don't cost as much as Ordoro. But when your store starts growing, it's a good idea to look for a robust inventory management system to help keep things neat, efficient and well automated *across all sales channels* so you may focus on more important things.

Quick Caveat: Some (if not all) of the Ordoro's integrations with other services will attract additional costs (at times recurring monthly fees) from the service providers. This is in addition to the $99 per month charged by Ordoro.

Xero

App/Service Name: Xero

Function: Business Accounting & Financial Management App

Price: From $20 - $40/Month

 Xero is a top-notch third party online business accounting and financial management service. It's actually a standalone tool that integrates with over 400 other eCommerce apps and platforms in addition to Shopify. Xero's feature-rich interface takes care of virtually all your stores' accounting needs. It addresses virtually all areas of your business accounting concern; from bookkeeping to invoicing and bank reconciliation to applicable tax calculations. It can easily be integrated into your inventory and bank account to ensure easy and automated work-flow.

Just like it was with Ordoro, new merchants can do without this tool at the initial stage. (Especially when you consider that the native Shopify system coupled with a few spreadsheets may be more than enough for a new small business wanting to test the ground). But Xero is definitely worth the investment as soon as you decide to scale things up. A wise man once said that "you don't grow big to manage well, rather you manage well to grow big". The only downside to this app is probably the fact that some folks may find its learning curve pretty daunting. But let's be honest here people, which accounting software is actually easy to learn?

Quick Tip: Shopify has developed a free app that integrates Xero into your store is a breeze, as long as you have a functional account with the service. You can find the app here.

Compass

App/Service Name: Compass

Function: Data Reporting and Benchmarking Tool

Price: Free (at the time of writing)

This is an amazing app. First of all, Compass aggregates all your store's essential data in one place. Then it crunches the entire data and shows you what your growth benchmark should be (based on the actual insight it gleaned from the other players in your industry). And finally, it gives you real-time recommendations on how to escalate your store's growth by optimizing some specific metrics such as Revenue, Traffic, Customer Acquisition Cost, and Customer Lifetime Value, etc. The recommendations are known to be super-specific. For example, while giving a recommendation to one merchant, this app actually said stuff like: *"Increase your* **Revenue** *by* **$75k** *by improving your* **25% Repurchase Rate** *by* **10%**".

Oh my, can it get any more specific than that?

Compass integrates with your eCommerce platform (Shopify), your traffic sources (Facebook and Google), and your payment gateway (Sprite). That's how it's able to gather and analyze all your essential data, build an authentic benchmark, and give you valid recommendations.

Quick Caveat: Compass requires access to Google Analytics (which is free) in order to function. And although Google Analytics is the web's go-to analytic engine, new merchants may find its interface a little bit too intimidating. If you're in that category, I'd recommend you start out with Hits Analytics, which is also free and a less complex alternative to Google Analytics.

Quick Tip: Hits Analytics has an inbuilt feature that allows you to create and deploy laser targeted and retargeted ads on Facebook and Google. This feature attracts a charge of 20% of your ad budget as a maintenance fee (if you decide to use it). A cheaper alternative is Vintage Analytics which charges 15% or less as your ad budget increases.

Recommended User Experience (UX) and Interaction Apps/Services
Tidio Live Chat
App/Service Name: Tidio Live Chat
Function: Live Interaction with Customers Across Multiple Channels

Price: Free - $24/Month

Tidio is an awesome app that makes it a breeze to have a live conversation with your store's visitors on multiple channels. You can run it on the web and on mobile (both iOS and Android) at a go. The mobile integration means that you're going to be available to your customers consistently even if you run a one-person team. And when you do go offline, the app will display an offline contact form on your store so visitors can leave you their messages. You can also set it up to show your visitors a predefined message on autopilot.

Impressively this app also lets you see what your store visitors are typing so you can get ready with your response before they even submit the message. It also gives you full access to a live list of your store's current visitors, including their languages and choice of browsers. The knock out feature is that the app is multilingual. This means that no matter what your store's default language is, your conversation with your visitors will be displayed to them in their respective languages. Tidio Live Chat also integrates with other apps, such as CRM, email marketing apps and help-desk tools, which makes it even more awesome.

RevampCRM

App/Service Name: RevampCRM

Function: Customer Relationship Management

Price: $19/Month

The rare beauty of RevampCRM is that it enables you to efficiently organize and segment your customers for effective marketing/sales communication. And to crown it all, the app is decisively crafted for Shopify, from the ground up. Nonetheless, RevampCRM is also a full-scale CRM in its own right. And, in addition to customer segmentation, it also handles the other core CRM stuffs like Contact Management, Leads Management; Sales follow up, Sales Management, Smart Email Sales Reporting, and Analysis, Email Marketing. Plus, the best part by far is, RevamCRM was actually built for online retailers and small business owners.

Quick Tip: The customer segmentation function of RevampCRM is a very essential feature you want to use to the fullest in your business. This is regardless of whatever CRM you eventually decide to go for. Segmenting your customers and relating with them smartly can be the difference between running a mediocre store and managing a soaring eCommerce brand that everyone wants to *repeatedly* do business with.

Quick Caveat: RevampCRM may be absolutely more than enough for most new Shopify store owners. But it may not be quite suitable if you are looking to scale your store into a huge brand that has a massive list of products in the near future. Thus it may be more reasonable to start out with any other CRM platforms that can easily accommodate your store's rapid growth with little or no upgrade issues. SalesForce is a good example of an enterprise-class CRM app.

LimeSpot

App/Service Name: LimeSpot

Function: User Experience Enhancement and Personalization Tool

Price: $0 - $135/Month

Okay, (at the time of this writing) LimeSpots's website interface sucks. And that's big time. But what the app lacks in image aesthetics it seems to have made up for in optimal functionality - a typical case of a product that's both made and *promoted* by hardcore geeks. But does anyone really care how the site looks as long as the app gets its job well done? And definitely, LimeSpot seems to be way up above and beyond other similar apps in Shopify App Store. And that's going by the ton of glowing community reviews it has attracted so far.

Good thing is, LimeSpot uses machine learning and its in-house patent-pending linguistic technology to create intelligent product-matching and recommendations for your customers based on their social media interests and overall web activities. This helps tremendously to boost customer engagements and sales in your store. Plus the app comes with flexible customization options and easy few clicks installation procedure on Shopify.

Quick Caveat: LimeStone is unlike many other Shopify apps. It has its own custom uninstall procedure. This means you'll have to go through a custom process to get it off of your store if you ever decide to quit using it. Trying to merely uninstall it the regular way may lead to some errors in your store's internal documentation. Fortunately, the app developer has a special tool that you may use to remove the app correctly.

Notify

App/Service Name: Notify

Function: Notification and Customer Engagement App

Price: $14.99/Month

Notify is a very popular Notification App amongst Shopify merchants. The impressive thing about the app is that it's very lean and efficient. It does not try to do too many things, but it does its own thing so well. For example, it makes exceptional use of the Social Proof concept. Some folks even reported seeing up to 100% hike in sales after deploying Notify to their respective stores.

Here's how it works: Say, for example, a visitor lands on your store from New York just at the time another customer from Toronto finished paying for a "Shiny Red Handbag". Notify will flash a cute alert to the new visitor, saying stuff like: "A customer from New York bought a "Shiny Red Handbag 2 minutes ago". This is a super-effective way to lure the new visitor into buying the same bag too (or any other product you may choose to highlight with Notify). The app is very customizable. And it's mobile-ready. In a nutshell, it's believed that Notify will increase your store's social proof, strengthen your first time visitor's confidence and increase your sales dramatically.

Quick Tip: For the most dynamic user experience and increased sales, try using Notify in conjunction with personalization apps like *LimeSpot* and selected user engagement and social proof apps. You also want to make sure to use a tool like *Abandon Aid* or *MoonMail Recover Checkouts* that will help reduce *cart abandonment rates* in your store and automatically recover sales that would have otherwise been lost when your customers get distracted at the point of purchase.

Magnify

App/Service Name: Magnify

Function: Multi-lingual Shopify Store App

Price: $17.50/Month

Okay, so Shopify was not originally designed to support multilingual Stores from its core. This is changing though, but the process is still quite slow and a bit complex. I guess that's because the demand for other core features seems to be way higher than the demand for native support for a *simultaneous* switch to multiple languages. Thus, up till the time of this writing, setting up a full-scale multilingual store on Shopify has remained an uphill task. The few available solutions were either tedious to implement or downright inefficient. This is where Langify comes in.

The app helps make things less messy if you decide to make your storefront available in other languages. It's important to understand that this is not just about translation. It's more about having different folks access your store in more than one language at the same time. A lot of things come into consideration here. For example, making the checkout page available in multiple languages and enabling search engine indexation (for each of the chosen languages), etc., are two of several other factors that are hard to crack when setting up a multilingual store. But Langify seems to have a viable workaround for the two scenarios and more.

Quick Caveat: Langify does not offer automatic translation. And it may not feature product prices in multiple languages without additional apps. This means you either have to do the translation yourself or hire someone else to do it. And for those of you that really want to build a multilingual store, *Localize* is another great multilingual app you may want to compare with *Langify.*

Minifier

App/Service Name: Minifier

Function: Image Size Minimizer and (in effect) Store Load Speed Enhancer

Price: 1¢ – 2¢/Image

How fast your store loads (especially on mobile devices) is one of the strong factors that will determine how well your shop will rank on search engines. Slow stores are annoying. And Google is totally aware of this one. So if your store doesn't load in *3 seconds* or less you'd probably find it a bit hard to impress your first-time visitors let alone staying on top of Google. But using un-optimized images is often the major factor that slows stores down. And that's where Minifier comes in. This app will trim down the weight of your images without distorting much of the image quality. Minifier optimization affects every graphic element in your theme to help ensure a store-wide speedy load time.

Quick Caveat: Note that un-optimized images alone are not the only reason sites get slow. Other factors may be at play too. For example, your store can become slow when you install too many apps. This is because each app will load its own assets into your theme. How your theme is designed can also be a factor for slowness. The browser, platform, and the internet connection through which your store is accessed can also drag things down. All or any combination of these factors can make a store slow.

Recommended Promotions Apps

SEO Manager

App/Service Name: SEO Manager

Function: On-Store Search Engine Optimization App

Price: $20/Month

Attracting enough chunks of targeted traffic to your online store is the biggest challenge that faces every eCommerce merchant. And proper SEO (search engine optimization) is a major way to confronting that challenge. Thus having your store on the coveted spots (on various search engine result pages) becomes one of the holy grails of eCommerce marketing. For starters, it brings a ton of free (and at times some laser targeted and cash-carrying) traffic to your store. And that's without saying that doing your store's SEO well enough can also transform your brand into a household name in your target market pretty quick.

But, as someone rightly pointed out, doing SEO for a regular website is way easier said than done. So when you bring an eCommerce storefront into the already too complex SEO trouble, the equation will simply get more complicated. And that's where SEO Manager comes in. This app helps you put your shop on the right on-store SEO route.

Quick Caveat: There's hardly any single tool that takes absolute care of all aspects of search engine optimization. So SEO Manager is not different in this regard. Thus despite its huge collection of features, it can only manage an on-store aspect of SEO. It has no features for link/mention and PR/relationship building. If you want any of those solutions for your store (and we all do) you'd just have to search them out either on the Shopify App Store or think of hiring a Shopify Marketing/SEO Expert.

Soundest

App/Service Name: Soundest

Function: eCommerce Email Marketing App

Price: $0 - $2k+/month

Email remains one of the most effective (yet cheapest) channels for personal and business communication. This means an email should be a foundational channel you use to communicate your brand messages and sell your products to your target audience. The thing with email is that it allows you to acquire, nurture and regain leads/customers like no other platform does, at least at the moment. Luckily, there are lots of apps you may use to wire up your online store for world-class email marketing. Soundest is one of the best picks when you compare such apps.

Soundest makes eCommerce email marketing easy. With Soundest you'll find that creating a new email campaign is as quick as picking which product to promote. It also has a good segmentation feature which makes it pretty easy to send very relevant messages to each group of your leads/customers. The apps' new Scratch Card feature means your email engagement rates are likely to go chart-shatteringly up. Thing is, Soundest is specifically built for eCommerce, and that alone makes a lot of difference. The only downside, however, is that it uses a loop pricing model which kind of kicks the cost up to as your usage grows. But it also has a *"free forever plan"* which allows you to send up to 15,000 emails per month.

BlogFeeder

App/Service Name: BlogFeeder

Function: Shopify Blog Syncing App

Price: $5.99/month (or $9.99 for a one-off use)

Another awesome thing about the Shopify platform is that each account comes preloaded with a full-scale blog engine. This means you can start blogging away right inside your store's back office, from day one. This is definitely huge good news for merchants who have zero blogging experience. But how about seasoned bloggers (especially on third-party platforms like Blogger and Tumblr etc.) with established followers who may want to monetize their various communities with an online store? That's where BlogFeeder comes in. With the app, you can import your content from any blogging platform right into your Shopify store with just a few clicks.

Quick Caveat: Using duplicate contents online comes with several SEO consequences which may also spillover on your brand. So, while the blog feed creators seem to have upped their game in so many ways, it's still wise that you weigh the pros and cons before deploying this app.

Quick Tip: If you're looking to position your store favorably on search engines in order to attract *new organic leads* to your store, then syncing your existing blog/community contents into your store (with a bit of technical workaround) may be a good idea. But if all you want is to sell your products to *your existing community,* then it might be a better idea to *take your store to that community* using a relevant sales channel. We'll talk more about sales channels shortly.

ShoppingFeed

App/Service Name: ShoppingFeed

Function: Product Syndicator for Multiple Marketplaces and Shopping Engines

Price: $10 - $39/month

No doubt, eCommerce is booming the world over. As a result, there's a plethora of shopping engines, marketplaces and advert channels out there waiting to be harnessed. But how do you get your products featured on some of these locations (over a thousand places actually) at once without turning some of your hairs blue overnight? ShoppingFeed (amongst others) is the answer. The app makes product syndication very easy. With up to a thousand channels across the globe, the options are simply so huge. Again, ShoppingFeed actually does more than syndicate your products across multiple channels. It also enables you to take orders across your chosen channels and still have your Shopify inventory updated in real-time.

Quick Caveat: Virtually all Shopping Engines will only list your products for a fee. Yet the traffic you get from them is typically made up of bargain hunters. This means that, unless you are listing a rare product that's not available elsewhere, you are most likely going to get into a price war with your competitors. And in this case, only the bargain hunters are the real winners.

Quick Tips: I do not recommend multi-channel syndication to brand new (small-scale) merchants. It's way better to try it only after you've garnered some good experience doing the basic stuff. But the decision is all yours to make, regardless.

to

App/Service Name: YotPo

Function: User Generated Content and Social Proof Generation App

Price: $0 - $699/month

According to a 2013 survey conducted by Dimensional Research, up to 90% of respondents say their buying decisions were influenced by online reviews, Marketing Land reports. The research also found that social media (Facebook in particular) was the leading source of positive reviews on the web. This goes to highlight the mind-blowing necessity of generating tons of verifiable social proofs for your online store. Of course, you may not totally be able to control how, when, and where the first or next *negative* reviews about your eCommerce site may pop up. But you sure cannot afford to wait for the *positive* reviews to happen.

In fact, the same survey revealed that *54%* of respondents shared bad business experiences with *more than five people*. But only *33%* admitted sharing good experiences with more than five people. This shows that up to *67%* of your shoppers *may* not share the good experiences they had in your store with many people (that's if they even share it at all) unless you *actively* inspire them to do so. It is this active inspiration and generation of social proofs that YotPo is created for. And seriously, I don't know another tool on Shopify App Store that does it better - at least not as at the time of this writing.

Coupon Pop

App/Service Name: Coupon Pop

Function: Coupon Based Promotion App

Price: $9.99/month

Coupons are powerful incentives. They make your customers and visitors take actions they may never take otherwise. Do you want to get more people to click the payment button, subscribe to the email list, or join your social network? You can achieve any or all of these just by offering your visitors and customers the right coupons at the right time. Coupon Pop makes the entire process easy and automatic. It's a straightforward plug-and-play system. The app integrates so well with many leading social networks and email marketing platforms. And that's so awesome, as it helps you drive leads to all segments of your sales funnel literally from all angles. The app actually boasts that it can help you increase sales by up to 33% each month.

Quick Caveat: Pop-Ups can get some folks seriously upset. And the last thing you want is to get your site visitors angry. So use this app with wisdom. Put user experience ahead of sales, and you will most likely end up with more sales in the long run.

Recommended Sales Channel Apps/Services

In the olden days, retailers would stock up their inventories, put up some fancy adverts (if they could) and hope that customers will **come** to buy their stuff. Fast forward to the current era, Shopify (and other eCommerce platforms) are gradually but consistently changing the way stores operate. Thanks to the idea of multiple sales channels. Now you can literally take your business to *all* the places where your customers are. And this is possible both offline and online. No doubt, that's much better than the old way of just staying in one location and hoping that your customers will come to meet you. Each Shopify account now comes preloaded with multiple sales channel apps that make it so easy to take your business to where your customers are.

Online Store Sales Channel

Quick Tip: To open the sales channels window, just click on *Settings* (at the left menu in your Shopify admin panel) and then click on *Sales Channels*.

By default, the *Online Store Sales Channel* is installed on your Shopify account from the moment it's set up. But you also have a bunch of other sales channels pre-bundled into your Shopify account and waiting to be put to use. For example, you can set up the *POS Sales Channel* right now and start selling your products in person (wherever you are) using your *iPad, iPhone* or *Android device*. It's that easy.

As at the time of this writing, Shopify has a total of seven native sales channels. I used the word *native* to reemphasize the fact that these sales channels are already part of all Shopify plans (minus the Shopify Lite) and are free to use. Of course, you don't have to use all of them from day one, but you should consider deploying each of them as soon as possible. And, as was also hinted early on, *Online Store* is the default sales channel followed by *POS*. But below is the list of the other five channels (just in case you want to check them out already).

• *Buy Button Sales Channel* - The Buy Button Sales Channel literally allows you to embed your products anywhere on the web where HTML is accepted. This could be on your *old blog post, forum discussion or email, etc*. And the best part is that anyone can do it. You can also customize your Buy Button to match the theme of the location you want to embed it on.

• *Facebook Sales Channel* - The Facebook Sales Channel allows you to embed a shop tab on your Facebook page. This means your customers can order your products directly from your store without leaving Facebook. This is the new norm.

• *Mobile App Sales Channel* - This one requires a bit of technical experience. As at the time of this writing, the Mobile App Sales Channel only allows you to sell *physical products* to your customers through your store's native app either on iOS or Android.

• *Twitter Sales Channel* - Just like the Facebook version, Twitter Sales Channel converts your regular tweet to a standalone store complete with a clear call to action. This means folks can buy your product from twitter without necessarily visiting your store. Twitter Sales Channel is only available to US merchants at the time of this writing.

• *Pinterest Sales Channel* - Shopify allows you to take your store to Pinterest too. This means your folks don't only have the option to *Pin* your stunning product image, they can now be prompted to *Buy It* too.

Quick Caveat: The availability of some sales channels (especially Twitter and Pinterest) is based on your store's currency, physical location, and type of products you sell. For more detailed information on each of these sales channels, see this Shopify article.

Last Thought On the Recommended Apps

Unless yours is a big brand with an unlimited budget, you probably don't want to upset your finance guy (or spouse) with a proposal to deploy all the recommended apps from day one. You just don't need to do that. It's better to pick a few that are most useful at the current stage of your store and then grow from there. Truth is, Shopify (without extra paid apps) is enough to get your store online and start generating new sales fast. That's the kind of result you should go for. You can start deploying the apps as your store begins to grow.

Quick Tip: Some of these apps may overlap in certain functions leading to a kind of redundancy. So it's important to research each paid app carefully and make sure it thoroughly meets your store's current needs (or those of the immediate future) before you click the Buy Button.

Quick Caveat: Although the creators of each of the recommended apps are also known for top-notch customer service, yet, it's worth mentioning that most of the apps are not native to Shopify. What that means is that the native Shopify support team may not be able to assist you if you ever run into problems regarding any third-party apps. So make sure to contact the app owners direct whenever there's a need for support.

Chapter 14 Build A Mailing List

Once you have finished setting up your store and getting your apps in place, it's time to start focusing on how to market your website and your product. Remember this simple rule: it doesn't matter how great your product is; if you don't market it, no one will find it.

This is a very simple rule that is worth guiding your entire marketing policy. Sometimes, we can get too caught up in how interesting and well-made our products are, to the point where we erroneously come to the conclusion that all we really need is a good product. However, there are extreme limits when it comes to things like word-of-mouth marketing. You need something stronger.

The mailing list is the single most powerful marketing tool that you should have in your arsenal. If you aren't working on building a mailing list, then you are going to be losing out on the ability to send specials, offers, and reminders to a potential customer base. Essentially, the mailing list comprises a list of people who have *voluntarily* handed their email addresses over to you. You are then free to email them as often as you like.

You need an email list because no other marketing system is as useful and direct as an email. All other forms of advertising rely on people noticing your ads and clicking on them, but an email arrives directly in their inbox and begs to be opened. There is no hoping to catch attention because unless they delete it without looking at it, they will read it, even if it's just for a moment.

Starting an email list isn't too difficult. There are plenty of different and unique services that you can utilize when it comes to building your mailing list. The one we would recommend would be MailChimp because it's intuitive, easy to use and free until you reach over 2,000 subscribers. MailChimp also lets you send custom campaigns and track the number of people who have opened, read and clicked on links within your emails. This kind of data is valuable because it allows you to know just how many people are engaging with your promotions.

Setting up an email list is easy, but getting emails on that list is the hard part. There are a variety of different ways that you can generate emails, but you'll want to be careful. Focus on getting quality emails, also known as leads. A quality lead is someone who is in your target demographic and would be interested in buying your product. One quality lead is better than 10 emails because you want to find emails that have a big chance of buying products from you. This means that you should develop email list building patterns composed only of high-quality leads who will actually purchase things from you. If you have 1,000 poor quality leads, you can email them until you're blue in the face, but you'll get lucky if even one person buys. However, if you had 100 high-quality leads, they might purchase far more because they are part of your target demographic.

So, if you are wanting to gain emails, you're going to need what is commonly referred to as a lead generation system. This means that you have some kind of attraction program in place that will gather leads for you. People don't just give their emails away; rather, they are cautious with their information until they come across a deal that is beneficial to them. Then, they are willing to trade their email in exchange for some kind of item.

The item can be a free product, a discount code, an eBook or any other thing of value. It's got to be valuable enough to encourage a potential customer to sign up, but not too valuable that it would attract people outside of your target demographic. For example, if you sold knitting patterns, you could have a free eBook with knitting patterns, which in turn would attract people who were into knitting. But if you were to offer a free crocheted hat, many people who find the product value but have no interest in knitting patterns would sign up for it. This costs you a lot of your money and, worst of all, doesn't provide you with much value.

One of the most tried and true methods of lead generation is the free eBook giveaway. You simply offer the eBook on your website in exchange for an email address. This is one of the best ways to start a relationship with a potential customer because the eBook will give them an opportunity to sample some of your work. If you aren't much of a writer, you can always hire a freelancer or a ghostwriter to make something for you. The book doesn't have to be really long; it just has to add some kind of value to your potential client's life.

Promotions, contests, and giveaways are all great ways to generate leads as well, but you should always make sure that they are only appealing to your target demographic. Going outside of your demo is a costly endeavor and is ultimately a waste of time. Instead, keep your focus on finding quality leads by developing good giveaways or, as they are called, lead magnets.

You might be wondering how exactly people are going to find out about your giveaways. You can have the best lead magnet in the world, but if people aren't landing on your website, then how are they going to hear about it?

Chapter 15 Expanding Your Product Line

Once you have finally gotten everything up and rolling there is nothing left to do but keep your nose to the grindstone and keeping marketing your store until you find success. Eventually, you are going to feel the need to begin expanding the types of products that your store sells, and in doing so you will open yourself up to many new questions and concerns.

Adding products tactically

The life cycle of the products on your page can be seen as being in one of four primary cycles. The startup phase is when a product first comes on the market and you are building awareness of it. The second is growth when sales of that particular product are growing the most; this is followed by maturity when the product begins to regularly sell an expected amount of units. Finally, the maturity stage is then sometimes followed by the exit stage is when the interest for the product is in a decline. While not every product hits all the stages, when a product begins to decline in sales you need to know what to do.

When you are ready to start expanding your stock, what you need to do is look at the analytics and determine just which of your products are producing the most consistent conversions. From there, it is simply a matter of analyzing the data and determining if adding another similar item would likely split the number of sales or if it is likely to double them. If this does not appear to be a step in the right direction, instead it might be better to determine why interest has dropped off on the product in question. Many of the common reasons for a product's decline have to do with a newer version being released or a change in the practices related to how that product is made or used. If this is the case, then something as simple as a few minutes' research can totally refresh your product line.

Find out what your customers want by including a survey regarding a product expansion in an email newsletter. There is nothing to be gained by beating around the bush in this instance and because only your best customers are likely going to interact with your newsletter, you have a way to directly ask your target audience what they want to buy from you. Take the time to draft up a realistic grouping of new products and also leave room for a write-in section, you may be surprised at the results you find.

Finding new products

When it comes to looking for new products to sell, the first thing you are going to want to do is to take a look at your existing stock and see if there are any obvious holes in your product line. If nothing sticks out to you at this point, your next best bet is likely to be to get offline and out into the world of brick and mortar retail stores. Take the time to seek out local variations on the theme of your niche and you might be surprised at how easily a new product idea or service comes to mind.

Back online, another viable alternative that more and more online stores are embracing is the world of Kickstarter manufacturers. Finding niche relevant content in this area is as easy as going to Kickstarter.com and looking through successfully funded Kickstarter pages to find products that might speak to your niche. Getting in touch with these types of manufacturers can often lead to a mutually beneficial relationship wherein they get a way to sell their product once they have delivered on their initial backer promises and you get an exclusive item that there is a proven demand for.

With that being said, it is important to ensure that the demand in question hasn't burned out with the fulfillment of the Kickstarter campaign, do some research and search out any additional demand or the product, the faster the better as if you don't meet the demand someone else will. While forming a good relationship with a Kickstarter manufacturer can lead to great things, it is important to do your research and only deal with manufacturers who have already successfully shipped product.

The great thing about Kickstarter is that anyone with an idea can get it funded, but this means that oftentimes people need to adapt to new roles on the fly which can be more difficult than it might first appear. Ensuring that the company has shipped product first will go a long way towards weeding out many of the problems inherent in the early days of a manufacturing company. Regardless, it is important to never offer to pay for exclusivity and to always get everything in writing as you will not be able to safely assume the company is not going to fold until they have sent you a few shipments of products.

Chapter 16 Legal Concerns

It is worth noting that I am not a lawyer, and the information in this chapter is generalized and should not be considered legal advice. You should check with a law professional to determine if there are any other legal concerns, what applies to your particular situation, and if there are any applicable laws or regulations based on your state of residence. That said, there are a few legal concerns worth considering on your own before you set off on your e-commerce journey or begin paying a legal professional.

Copyright and Intellectual Property

It should go without saying that you must follow all copyright laws when selling products in an e-commerce setup through Shopify. However, there is often some confusion about what is allowed and what falls under the concept of "fair use." Let's clear that up.

If you do not own the copyright to a product, trademark, image, or other materials, you cannot utilize it for profit without express permission from the creator or the proper licenses. This especially extends into many areas of design.

An obvious example includes the use of another company or person's intellectual property. Take Nintendo's ever-popular character, Mario. Despite the massive amount of products online that use his image, a vast majority of them are technically breaking copyright laws by infringing on Nintendo's trademark character. Without obtaining the proper licensing, placing his image on a t-shirt, mug, poster, notebook, or any other product is technically illegal. This applies even if you drew your own representation of the character. While this type of infringement is often overlooked, it is completely possible for Nintendo to sue you for essentially stealing from them. The same is true for other video game characters, cartoons, movies, etc.

With ebooks, videos, and other digital content, it is obviously copyright infringement to download these items and resell them without first getting permission. Not only is this illegal, but customers tend to frown upon sellers that don't do any of the work for themselves.

Likewise, despite the popular act of simply finding images on Google Images and using them on your design projects, it is crucial that any images you use are either in the public domain or you've paid for a license to use them. This also applies to things like fonts, clip art, design elements, etc. It is a huge misconception that simply because a font may be free to download that it's also free to use for commercial products. If you're not using a font that comes with your computer, it's wise to take the time to determine if you are required to purchase a license to use it. As a rule of thumb, if you're unsure if you're breaking any copyright law, just avoid that particular element, image, etc.

Business Licenses

Not all e-commerce sellers require a business license, but it depends on many factors. First, you should check your state's laws regarding e-commerce and business licenses. Second, if you plan to have any salaried or hourly employees, you will need to obtain a business license and an employer identification number for tax purposes. (It is worth noting that you can hire independent contractors without an employer identification number.)

For those of us that don't need a business license, we will be considered "sole proprietors," and that means that we will generally be the only "employee" in our business. This also means that our personal finances and business finances are intermingled, and as such, our taxes are as well. For this reason, it may be advantageous to obtain a business license even if you don't plan on working with employees. Should you use credit to build your business and have to default on loans or declare bankruptcy, this will be personal bankruptcy instead of business bankruptcy, which will harm your financial health for years to come.

Taxes

As a general piece of advice, you have to pay your taxes.

That said, with online sales, the general rule for federal taxes is that you must claim your earnings in full if you've made more than 200 transactions and netted $20,000 or more in sales. Unless you're still a fledgling seller with a full-time job on the side, it is safe to assume we should just claim our earnings regardless of meeting these criteria.

As mentioned above, if you have employees working under you, you must have an employee identification number, and you must report your employee's earnings. You will be responsible for issuing W-2s for employees. For independent contractors, you will be required to issue 1099-MISC forms if you have paid them over $600 within the year.

It is wise to have a tax professional sit down with you and walk you through all of the ins and outs of taxes as either a business or a sole proprietor. Doing your own taxes may save you a few dollars, but the likelihood of being audited rises dramatically for self-employed individuals that fail to handle the process correctly.

Some states require that you charge sales tax for buyers within the same state as well.

Privacy and Spam

Did you know that it is actually illegal to spam? To put that into perspective, it is illegal to push products in an unsavory way. This doesn't mean you should forego emailing customers; in fact, email lists are a great way to increase sales and market your new products. When you make a sale or if you have someone sign up for an email list, it is alright to email them, you just need to take a few steps to ensure you avoid falling into the "spam" category.

First, all of your messages should be clearly marked as advertisements. Second, the text within the subject line and body of an email shouldn't be misleading whatsoever. Lastly, you need to offer a method for customers to unsubscribe from receiving messages from you. Ideally, you will also include a legal postal address within all of your messages as well, even if it's just a PO Box.

As an online retailer, you're sometimes privy to quite a bit of information concerning your customers, including contact information, postal address, full name, and much more. While it may be tempting to sell this information or use other methods of taking advantage of it, it is highly illegal, and the fines and potential jail time are far more damaging than the meager earnings a few scams offer. Just don't do it.

State Laws

I've mentioned it briefly, but it is important to understand that some states have their own laws regulating how e-commerce and running a business in that state must be handled. Take the time to research your state laws, talk with legal professionals, and make sure to utilize this knowledge to avoid potential issues.

Reminder!

This is not a complete list of legal issues, but it is a brief starting off point to help you avoid the most common legal mistakes new entrepreneurs find themselves making. It is highly advised to seek legal counsel and do your own research regarding the potential legal issues surrounding your business.

Chapter 17 Simplicity at Its Best

Whether you have a B2B business realm or a B2C model, you need a platform that does more than the normal software functions such as transactions. A comprehensive model such as Shopify will make you competitive in the fast-paced and robust markets present now. It can provide the significant advantage you need over your competitors who do not have the support of similar technology.

Shopify supplies you with the tools you need to build your store online. Once you know the basic setup, which is easy to master, you can expect a seamless functioning of the store. And you have 24/7 phone or online support from the service. So, creating an e-commerce site for your business is just a breeze with Shopify. You will not need to know any technical codes or other background knowledge to set up your store online.

An overview of Shopify

Shopify is one of the best e-commerce shopping carts that is completely web-based. With Shopify, you will be able to sell your services or goods online in an effective manner. All the aspects of an online store set up such as building a website, choosing the right design, customizing the site to fit your brand and products, managing orders and customers, tweaking the various features, receiving reports on sales, etc., are streamlined and easier to deal with when you use Shopify.

Shopify is a feature enriched sales register appropriate for small and big online retailers. The best thing about the software is you need not spend towards maintaining servers of your own, as the software is taken care of by Shopify's servers. This effectively curbs all the efforts and costs involved in server maintenance.

Founded in the year 2006, Shopify has its headquarters in Ontario, Canada. It was originally developed by Daniel Welland, Scott Lake and Tobias Lutke for the snowboarding business they owned together. The idea for Shopify was born, when they required a shopping cart with better features than what was available at that time. They designed their own solution that met with all their requirements. The efficacy of the software made them decide on marketing it. Soon Shopify became a very popular and trusted service in the e-commerce shopping cart segment.

At present, Shopify serves over 243,000 merchants and the businesses using the service are continuously growing. Shopify has clients such as Amnesty International, Github, Foo Fighters, etc. The company has done transactions that amount to more than $14 billion.

While the original version was very popular, the subsequent version Shopify 2, launched in the year 2013, surpassed the reputation of the earlier version as a highly effective e-commerce platform. The newer version had strong merchant minded and cleaner backend features. The Live Theme Editor feature and the enhanced search and filter features added to the service further increased its effectiveness. Other highlights of Shopify 2 include improved analytics, better reporting tools and facility to issue part of the refunds, instead of doing the transaction via PayPal.

Convenience and simplicity

Although Shopify has numerous features in it, you need not be overwhelmed. The system is structured logically. The entire set up of your online store is easier without any complicated procedures. You will need just a few minutes to set up the basic store. Other than the designing aspect, which needs some attention because you need to balance the colors for the theme at the backend, Shopify is quite an easy to use service. Once the basic store is built, you can easily add on to it to create a fantabulous store.

Exclusive features

Some important features that make Shopify an excellent option are:

- You can put your online store to a trial run before you launch it officially. This trial run is done in two ways. One is through a live editor feature and the other way is doing it online.

- To own a domain name for your store, you can do it easily via the Shopify dashboard. This is quick and easy when compared to other services, which make it mandatory to purchase the domain via third party services.

Customer-facing or front end features

A convenient and easy to use interface is one of the significant features a shopping cart should have. A customer should be able to navigate through the site smoothly, select the items needed, buy them and complete the transaction successfully.

If on the other hand, the process is frustrating, it will be difficult for the customer to buy a product, even if it is a good one. Thus with a difficult navigation feature, you will be left with numerous abandoned carts. And to make matters worse, customers will definitely not return to the site, nor will they recommend the store to others.

When you consider Shopify, it excels in the convenience feature. It is very easy to build a store using Shopify. Managing is also a breeze. Both in terms of administration and customer-facing end, the software is easy to manage.

Customers who transact through a site backed by Shopify will feel assured about the business. They would consider the business to be a well-organized, professional and legitimate retail establishment. And one of the best and most admired parts of using Shopify software is, you will not find any of its brandings in your site, leaving a very consistent and great shopping experience.

Administration Panel or Back end management

For building your online store, you need just a few minutes. You can easily open and build the basic structure of your online store. From the beginning stage, you have the facility to preview your site, so you will know how it will look like before you launch it live. This can be done using the live editor backend feature or by a password online. The password is sent to you via email after you sign up for the free trial version.

To make the entire process easier, you are guided on the right way to use the present URL of your store. The domain set up mentioned earlier also helps a great deal. You can find this feature, when you click on the Store Settings and opt for a domain.

The admin homepage provides you with four important steps. These steps help you to create the necessary groundwork before you begin selling. These include

1. Adding products

2. Customization of brand

3. Domain set up

4. Deciding on shipping and taxes information

While these are the basic steps, there are other steps to consider too such as creating store policies, including a description of your shop and the details of the product, add on features such as Google Analytics, and others.

Features such as customer information, images, items, categories, and other related options are very direct and easy to understand. Partial returns and enhanced fraud detection features of the updated software version further make the software more effective.

Customer satisfaction

When it comes to shopping online, simplicity is vital. If a retail business has to invest more time in learning the basic set up and management of its store, it would start looking for an efficient and manageable shopping cart option. Shopify scores in this aspect, as it is easy to lay the groundwork with the software. The service is created in an efficient way, so you are able to tweak the features later on without having to do everything at the initial stage itself.

Outstanding user-friendly features

Other than the above-mentioned advantages of Shopify, here are a few more:

You can add products easily when compared to the competitors

It is easy to include links in the navigation menu for rearranging them

The article or blog section feature available with the standard Shopify format is a good one. You can add blog posts or pages easily.

Themes can be edited in a simple way.

What you need to have

As Shopify is an e-commerce software that is web-based, your requirements are very simple. You need to have a proper internet connection. For the software to function smoothly, an updated and current browser such as Safar, Firefox or Chrome is necessary.

While the operating system or hardware requirements are not much elaborate, if your system has updated technology, it would facilitate easier set up of your online store. In case, you are in need of hardware addition at your physical retail store, the service has retail packages for hardware, which it supports fully.

When you go through all the convenient and easy to use features you will understand that Shopify has made its platform as easy as possible without compromising on the innovative features, which are needed for customers to have a competitive edge.

Chapter 18 Shopify Tips and Tricks

Tips and tricks are always great for anything new that you are learning- it makes us do things better, more efficiently, in less time and achieve better results. Here are 8 tips to master your online business:

Going Premium with Themes

Themes are the backbone of your site and free themes only take you a certain distance in your business goals. Shopify is known for its amazing all-in-one themes that are contemporary, classy, and crisp, and using these make your store more upscale than the price tag of your theme. Speaking of the price tag, it is worth to invest in the theme of your choice just so that your store stands out from everyone else's.

Making your store beautiful will attract sales. Not only that, investing in premium themes enables your e-commerce site to be seamlessly functional but they also tell your brand story. The need to invest in the theme of your choice is crucial because it represents the look and feel of your products and your customers will have a more pleasurable experience browsing and buying products of your site.

Premium themes can make your store exclusive so this is a wise investment especially if you see your site growing.

Keep your eye on the ball

Your main goal is to create profits right? So that should be your focus. Do not get carried away by flashy graphics and so call 'must-haves' for your website or even long content that apparently 'speaks' to your audience. You do not want to lengthen the time it takes for your customers to decide to purchase your product. The idea is to get them to your site, browse for what they want, click on the product, read a short description and click on Add to Cart > Proceed to Checkout. Keep things moving forward and avoid anything that detracts from this mission.

Practice SEO

Part of your marketing should also be SEO. SEO is not dead so long as keywords are still used to search for anything and everything on the internet. You need to use SEO wisely not only on your website but also on your social media which is from content, titles, tags, image tags, descriptions- the whole nine yards. You will be found much easier through specific keywords.

Think like a customer

One of the reasons why you need to stick to a niche that you know and one that you are passionate about is so you understand customer pain points. What do you look for when you are on someone's website? What do you expect to find there? What kind of buying process makes you feel you purchase things fast? What makes you like the website you usually purchase from? Knowing the pain points yourself makes you understand what your customers want and how your product can help them accomplish their needs.

Product Reviews

The best way for any customer to know that the products that they are purchasing value for money are by reading reviews. Customers will click on products that have higher ratings and the likelihood of them purchasing it is if has good reviews and high ratings.DO not cheat on your reviews. If you have a product that always gets bad reviews- trash it. When you do, let your customers know that you are discontinuing it because this will help increase their confidence in your site. The fact that you have heard them and you are doing something about it increases brand trust.

Mix your marketing

There are many ways to reach your customers depending on who they are and what they do. For most e-commerce marketing methods, social media marketing and email marketing is the way to go. But you should not rely on it entirely. On and off, it is also good to meet with your customers and see who they are. Give product giveaways, hold online workshops or seminars, have an online meet-and-greet, feature your customers using your product or give them a shout out!

Make your logistics work well

Have strong and clear agreements on any potential logistical issues that you may encounter in your e-commerce business. Outline these in your contract and also have this on your website. Inform customers what to do if they have returned. Outline this with your supplier as well and establish standard operating procedures for returns, damaged items and so on. Outline what the shipping costs are as well between yourself and the supplier and what is the expected delivery date for your items between supplier and customer.

Establish your relationship with your supplier

Establishing and maintaining close relationships with your suppliers ensure that you can also extend the benefits to your customers. When your supplier trusts you, there will be many things that you can get done such as offer personalized packaging to your customers, ensuring speedy shipping, have lesser time in managing any issues you have to deal with if there are any delays. Collaboration is based on trust and the soonest you establish trust, the better.

Communicate your Product Strategy

Strong product descriptions ensure higher success rates of purchasing. This information is critical to your customer- they want to know what they are buying and the better you describe your product, the faster it would be for your customers to make a purchasing decision. Do not give long and vague descriptions and also do not put on duplicate content. Duplicate content will be penalized by search engines.

Using Apps that are Necessary

Apps bring in immense value to your site and that is what store owners on Shopify love about the platform. The value and power of your site rest not only in the design and content but also the add-ins you place to make the user experience powerful. These apps help you automate shipping information, scheduling, sending out emails, managing your inventory as well as your purchase orders. In short, it helps you save time as well as money.

That said, not all worth paying for or investing in it so you need to know which are worth to invest in and which apps are great as free versions. In order for you to do that, here are some tips:

- Research the kinds of apps that store owners are talking about and then test them out yourself. If they work great for others, chances are they will work excellently well for you too.

- Apps usually offer free trials before you sign up, so use the trial period to gauge if this app is what you need before you make a commitment.

- Be careful where your money goes because monthly subscription fees for your app may cause a dent into your monthly budget but if it does give you more sales, then the app is worth it. It is good to stick with an app on a monthly basis for a few months to know whether it helps with your store before committing to a yearly plan.

Maximize your PPC ROI

The Pay-Per-Click PPC game is ensuring that you use the right keywords to attract the right audience using the content that you place in your pages, especially your landing pages. PPC is a must-have strategy when it comes to e-commerce.

Use PPC to publicize your new products as well as drive traffic to your deals and offers. Optimize your PPC by ensuring that you use the right keywords at the right products or pages.

Shopify also assists new store owners by giving them extra AdWords credit so use this wisely. Store owners get about $100 for AdWords whenever you spend $25 on Shopify so to ensure that you get the most of this, you also need to work on creating a viable content and marketing strategy.

PPC's success relies entirely on conversions and social media is one of the ways that you can grow your source of revenue. Think about using these channels to engage and direct your target market to your site.

Keeping your business Online

You can take the stress out of selling by running your business on the go, using Shopify's mobile app. Use the app and save yourself some time as push notifications to your mobile ensures that you can always keep tabs on your sales figures as and when you need to.

Online business is great with Shopify as you can run your business with the flexibility of time and space- literally anytime, anywhere.

You can also make your business work for you by taking it on the road, using the mobile app. Speak to suppliers, update your store, check on inventory and many more without having the need to be in your office space.

Conclusion

Thank you for making it through to the end of Shopify.

The next step is to stop reading and to get started doing whatever it is that you need to do in order to ensure that you and those you care about will be properly taken care of in financial sense through you achieving your e-commerce goals. If you find that you still need help getting started you will likely have better results by creating a plan that you hope to follow including strict guidelines for various parts of the endeavor as well as the overall achievement of your goal(s) using guidelines from this book.

Studies show that complex tasks that are broken down into individual pieces, including individual deadlines, have a much greater chance of being completed when compared to something that has a general need of being completed but no real-time table for doing so. Even if it seems silly, go ahead and set your own guidelines and deadlines to monitor progress, complete with indicators of success and failure. After you have successfully completed all of your required steps, you will be glad you did.

Once you have finished your initial preparations it is important to understand that they are simply that, only part of a larger plan of preparation. Your best chances for overall success will come by taking the time to learn as many vital skills as possible. Only by using your prepared status as a springboard to greater heights will you be able to truly rest, for just a short while nonetheless, soundly knowing that you are headed in the right direction.

CPSIA information can be obtained
at www.ICGtesting.com
Printed in the USA
BVHW060137210222
629616BV00003B/125

9 781801 153706